The City Different and The Palace

The Palace of the Governors:
Its Role in Santa Fe History

By
Rosemary Nusbaum

Including Jesse Nusbaum's Restoration Journals

SUNSTONE
PRESS

SANTA FE

Book and Cover Design — Douglas Jerrold Houston

Printed in the United States of America

Library of Congress Cataloging in Publication Data

Nusbaum, Rosemary, 1907-
    The City Different and the palace.

    1. Santa Fe, N.M. Palace of the Governors.
I. Title.
F804.S28P346   978.9'56   78-17591
ISBN 0-913270-79-2

Published in 1978 by The Sunstone Press
Post Office Box 2321, Santa Fe, New Mexico 87501

TO THE MEMORY OF JESSE NUSBAUM

Of Jesse it can be said:

He was young, vigorous, and willing. Photographing not only his own, but the work of those about him, helping to save for people their heritage of antiquity, he typified the finest in the professions he followed and in his devoted love for the American West.

Rosemary.

LAUREATE

Here is my corporeal dwelling place — New Mexico
Fortunate my days in this enchanted land
Soft is the Sun on my adobe home.

I would be in each night, star-lit, read tomorrow's plans
And need not happiness beyond today's.

I would my spirit's dwelling place be here — New Mexico
That I might be one with your every season's change.

My corporeal self pulsating with your breast
My spirit one with all the elements.

Rosemary Nusbaum

FOREWORD

For nearly two and one-half centuries, until about 1850-60, it appears that Santa Fe, like Topsy, just grew naturally. Irrigation ditches diverting water from the Santa Fe River for nearby tillable fields largely determined the pattern of settlement and the development of roads up-river and down-river from the region of principal settlement adjacent to the Plaza. Commerce which developed first over the Chihuahua Trail, then the Santa Fe Trail, extended settlement outward from the Plaza along these historic trail approaches.

Through all this period of development, a simple regional type of architecture persistently prevailed. The Spanish settlers introduced the adobe brick and merged certain features of Pueblo Indian construction with such traditional forms of their colonial architecture as native materials permitted. Until about 1850, Santa Fe appears to have remained completely indifferent to non-regional architectural trends. After about 1850, a slow, insidious trend toward non-conforming architecture developed. The American Military occupation introduced the saw mill, and sawed lumber, fired brick, and new forms of roofing that altered appearances were slowly observed. Next, wealthy traders and other residences began to build ornate, non-conforming houses like those then in vogue in the East.

The advent of the Santa Fe Railroad in the early 1880's ended the excessive cost of importing materials over the Santa Fe Trail, and soon Santa Fe was indulging in all sorts of building innovations. This foreign architectural trend culminated alarmingly in the first decade of the present century with the introduction and rapid development of varied types of California bungalow in several sections of Santa Fe—vacant until then, or occupied by historic structures that could have readily been adapted to modern living needs.

In the midst of all this change, one historic structure remained true to its original form: the Palace of the Governors, still standing at the heart of the city and reflecting much of Santa Fe's glorious past. This book is a tribute to that edifice, and to the memory of Jesse Nusbaum, who played such an important part in retaining the historic character of the Palace.

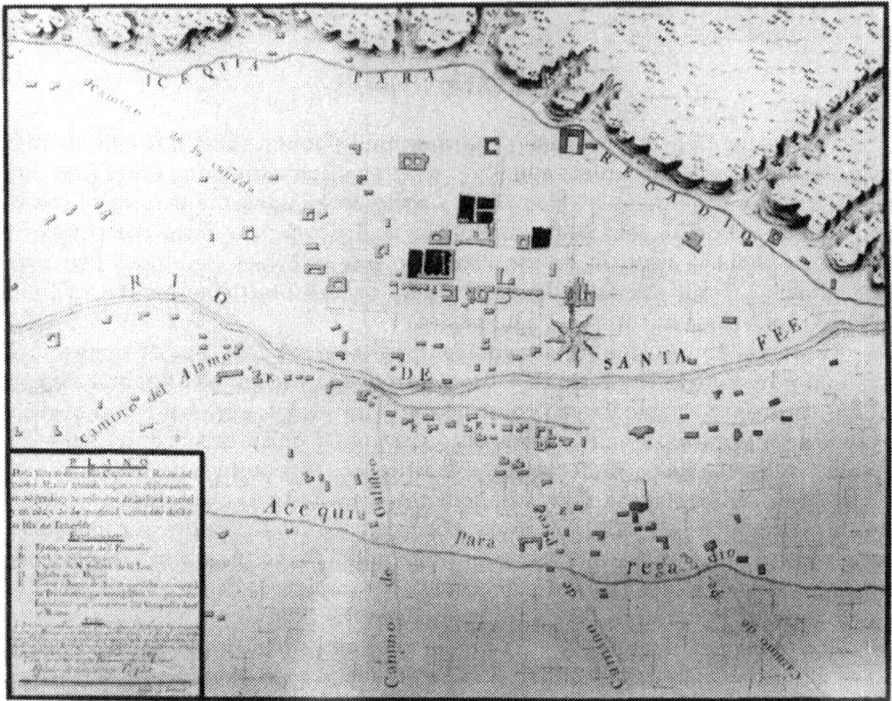

Called the José Urrutia map of Santa Fe, 1766-68.

Copy — British Museum Map of Santa Fe.

Photo of map by Jesse Nusbaum - 1912.

Nusbaum writes: "This map and the korbel was what I positioned the East and West ends of the Palace thereon."

Earliest known map of Santa Fe, drawn by Second Lieutenant José Urrutia who had accompanied the Marqués de Rubi, on a tour of inspection of the northern frontier presidios 1766-68, for Spain.

Miss Barbara Freire-Marreco, who had been at Canyon de Los Frijoles Summer session in 1910, with the newly established School of American Archaeology. Miss Freire-Marreco had come over from her teaching post as Fellow and Lecturer, Summerville College, Oxford University (Ethnology of the Pueblos) to join the Summer School at Frijoles.

When she went back she found the map in the British Museum. She sent a copy to Jesse and he photographed it and returned it . . . to her. This is the developed copy of his 5x7" glass negative.

THE ROYAL PALACE AT SANTA FE

CHAPTER I

New Mexico is thought to have received its name in 1565 from Ibarra, who called the country north of the settled Mexican provinces *un otro* or *Nuevo Mejico*.

Following Ibarra's expedition, there were a number of ill-fated attempts to explore and settle New Mexico. The first successful expedition was that of Don Juan de Oñate, a wealthy mine owner of Zacatecas, and son of a pioneer. The Spanish government, unable and unwilling to finance Oñate's proposal, granted him a contract September 21, 1595, when he offered to equip an expedition at his own expense.

After numerous delays, the army of soldiers and settlers, numbering about 400, a baggage and supply train of 83 wagons and carts, and 7,000 head of stock, left Santa Barbara for the north on February 7, 1598. On April 30, Oñate took formal possession of New Mexico at a point on the Rio Grande just below El Paso del Norte. Near Mount Robledo, Oñate started ahead with a small escort to examine the country. On July 11, he established the first Spanish capital in New Mexico at the Tewa village of Yugeuingge (called Yunqueyunque by Coronado) on the west bank of the Rio Grande, christening it San Juan, adding *de los Caballeros* (St. John of the Gentlemen) "in memory of those noble sons who first raised in these barbarous regions the bloody tree upon which Christ perished for the redemption of mankind" (Villagra, *Historia del Nuevo Mejico*). The main body of colonists, following more slowly, crossed the dread Jornado del Muerto (Journey of Death), and arrived five weeks later at San Juan, thus establishing the first permanent colony in New Mexico and the second in the United States (the first being San Augustine, Florida 1565).

Work on the first Spanish irrigation ditch was begun August 11, 1598, and on the first church in New Mexico, August 23. The church was dedicated on September 8 to San Juan Bautista. The next day Pueblo chiefs of the region agreed to receive Christian missionaries. The province was divided into seven mission districts, with eight Franciscan friars.

That first winter in New Mexico was fraught with hardships. Friendly Indians could not provide sufficient food for the colonists and mutiny developed among the soldiers. The colony stood firm only because of the courage of its pioneers.

The settlement referred to as San Juan Bautista, was later (about 1601) called San Gabriel del Yunque. San Juan de los Caballeros was generally used to denote the Tewa Pueblo on the east bank of the Rio Grande, to which the Indians had moved. The Spanish capital remained at San Gabriel del Yunque until the seat of government was removed to Santa Fe in the winter of 1609-10.

On December 4, the Acoma Indians revolted, trapping Oñate's nephew, Juan de Zaldivar, and eighteen of his men in their famous "Sky City" on the mesa.

Zaldivar, ten other soldiers, and a few servants were killed. To punish the Acomas, Oñate sent Vincente de Zaldivar, brother of the murdered Juan, with a hand-picked force to recapture the pueblo. The battle began January 22, 1599, and raged until January 24, when the Spaniards gained the mesa-top and were victorious. Setting fire to the pueblo, they sent the inhabitants to settle on the plains below. This ended organized resistance to Oñate, and on December 24, 1600, relief forces from New Spain reached San Gabriel.

Oñate left San Gabriel for Quivira, June 23, 1601, to visit that section, going probably as far west as the present Wichita, Kansas, and traversing sections covered by Coronado sixty years before. During his absence, settlers, soldiers, and all of the missionaries except one friar abandoned San Gabriel for the Santa Barbara mines or elsewhere. When Oñate returned on November 24, the settlement was all but abandoned. Vincente de Zaldivar followed the colonists, secured new missionaries and settlers, brought back some of the deserters, and San Gabriel flourished again.

Oñate, ever restless, set out for the South Seas (Pacific Ocean) on October 7, 1604, with thirty horsemen and two priests. He reached the Gulf of California on January 25, 1605, and took possession for Spain. The party started back to San Gabriel, saving themselves from starvation on the way by killing and eating their horses. On the return trip Oñate left his name on Inscription Rock, now El Morro National Monument, adding the date, April 16, 1605, instituting a practice followed by subsequent governors, soldiers, and priests.

Extensive expeditions, campaigns, and the exacting duties of governor had worn Oñate out, while huge expenditures from his own private fortune reduced him to poverty. Reinforcements for the colony were not forthcoming from Mexico City. A secret report on Oñate reached Philip III of Spain, and on June 7, 1606 he ordered Oñate to make no more explorations. In despair, Oñate resigned on August 24, 1607. The viceroy chose Juan Martinez de Montoya, one of Oñate's captains, as governor, but the colonists would not permit him to serve. Again they elected Oñate, but he declined to serve, so they chose his son Don Cristobal.

Sometime before March 5, 1609, the viceroy appointed Don Pedro de Peralta governor, with instructions to found a new capitol. During the winter of 1609-10, Peralta moved the settlers from San Gabriel to Santa Fe and carried out his orders which were "To designate one block of the streets for the erection of the Royal Houses." He built his government headquarters fronting on a plaza. The dominant structure was the Palace of the Governors.

At the same time one of the earliest Church leaders to assume leadership of the Franciscans was Fray Isidro Ordoñez, who claimed to have come from the King with an order (which may have been spurious) to the effect that those colonists desiring to return to Mexico might do so. The depletion of the colony left Peralta unimpressed and the fight was on. When Ordoñez attempted to interfere with the dispatch of troops to Taos Pueblo to collect tribute, he was over-ruled by Peralta and the Governor was excommunicated and ultimately imprisoned by agents acting for Ordoñez. Peralta was returned to Mexico under guard and Ordoñez later found himself before the Holy Office of the Inquisition.

Exploitation of the Indians by friars and governors in the form of imposed labor or tribute continued, and the Indians' resentment of the suppression of their religion led to a series of sporadic uprisings beginning in 1640. The immediate cause for the first uprising was the whipping, imprisoning, and hanging of forty Indians who would not give up their religion. In 1643 the Jemez Indians were discovered plotting with the Navaho to drive the Spaniards from New Mexico; and in 1650, the Pueblos of Jemez, Isleta, Alameda, San Felipe, and Cochiti conspired with the Apache for the same purpose. These uprisings and the Apache outbreak of 1676, with the leaders and participants in each instance hanged, imprisoned or sold into slavery, culminated finally in the Pueblo Revolt of 1680, led by Po-pé.

Po-pé was a Tewa Indian medicine-man and native of San Juan pueblo. He persuaded the Pueblos that their gods had ordered the revolt and that all Spaniards must be expelled or killed. The religion of the Pueblo Indians was based upon age-old myths and rituals that dictated almost every act of their lives; and for those who had been converted to the Christian faith the throwing aside of the new teachings was not difficult. With the expulsion of the Spaniards, the native beliefs prevailed, and Catholic churches were destroyed. It was not until Diego de Vargas reconquered New Mexico in 1692 that the Roman Catholic Church was re-established.

The Palace of the Governors in Santa Fe was apparently a structure of considerable size at the time of the Pueblo Revolt. The walled and fortified Casas Reales were big enough to house more than a thousand persons, 5,000 head of sheep and goats, 400 horses and mules and 300 head of beef cattle, without crowding. The great thickness of the Palace walls indicates that the building was a place of refuge and defense. It was almost as solid as concrete, poured and puddled into one piece, a technique typical of pre-Columbian time, although walls were probably built and rebuilt by Indians after the Revolt (Nusbaum in his restoration of 1909-13, left a small section under glass in a main wall). Upon these earliest puddled walls were laid adobe bricks in the manner the Spaniards taught the Indians. (Nevertheless, even this building was once trimmed and modernized to the extent of including a delicate Victorian balustrade across the length of the parapet.)

The Pueblo Indians planned with Apache aid to murder or expel all Spaniards and to destroy Santa Fe. On August 9, two days before the time set for the uprising, the plot was discovered by Governor Antonio de Otermin. Apprised of this discovery, the Indians began the rebellion in the early morning hours of August 10. Their surprise attack resulted in the deaths of more than four hundred Spaniards, including twenty-one priests, north of Santa Fe. Settlers near Santa Fe gathered at the Casas Reales, preparing for a last stand. Indian hordes sent the governor two crosses, one white and one red. If he returned the white and promised to abandon the country, the Spaniards might go in peace. If red they promised to massacre them all. The Spaniards chose to fight and sent back the red cross. The Indians then cut off Santa Fe's water supply and began the siege. Starvation soon threatened the Spanish, who early on August 20 attacked the sleeping Indians, killing three hundred and taking forty-seven captive.

The Palace was a house of desolation for thirteen years under the Pueblos. It was here that a thousand men, women and children huddled together under Otermin and watched the angry hordes as they drew ever nearer, hurling death and destruction. Two fugitives from Taos heard the boom of the cannon from the "torreons," or towers, and saw flames of the burning chapel and glow of the smoldering ruins of the Casas Reales, on the day that Otermin and his dejected, half-clad band started for El Paso del Norte, abandoning the conquests of a hundred years.

When the Spaniards had gone, the Pueblos destroyed all previous official records, tore down and burned churches, washed baptized Indians with amole (soapweed) in the Santa Fe River to cleanse them of the stain, and annulled Christian marriages.

After several abortive attempts to re-enter Santa Fe Don Diego de Vargas Zapata Lujan Ponce de Leon arrived on September 13, 1692 with an army of three hundred men from El Paso. The Indians surrendered peacefully before nightfall. Without losing one man the royal banner of Spain was raised once again over the Palace of the Governors on September 14th, 1692, repossessing the country for the viceroy. But De Vargas the reconquerer was thrown into a dungeon in the Palace by the envious marplot Cubero, and it was only after three years of imprisonment that he was restored to power.

On this site innumerable historic gatherings have taken place. Over one hundred governors and captains-general have occupied the Palace—Spanish, Pueblo, Mexican, and both Confederate and Union Americans, beginning with Peralta and ending with Territorial Governor George Curry in 1909. Some of them had claimed sovereignty as far east as the Mississippi, west to the Pacific Coast, and south as far as the present city of Parral, in the Mexican state of Chihuahua. No other building in the United States links the historic past with the present as does the Palace. It is a story of past cultures told in puddled walls, adobe bricks, and plaster.

The time of caravans with goods and settlers passed and the trail which came to be known as "El Camino Real" (The Royal Highway), coming from El Paso del Norte would never again be described as Josiah Gregg did in his *Commerce of the Prairies*: "The arrival of the caravan always was productive of great excitement among the natives. 'Los Americanos! Los Carros! La entrada de la caravana!' were to be heard in every direction. Crowds of women and boys flocked around to see the newcomers . . . . Each wagonner must tie a brand new 'cracker' to the end of his whip, for on driving through the streets and the *plaza pública* everyone strives to outvie his comrades in the dexterity with which he flourishes this badge of authority."

Caravans were unloaded after being cleared at La Garita and the tribute paid at La Fonda, the inn at the end of the trail, under the gaze of dark girls who hid their faces under lace mantillas, lounging soldiers from the barracks, and expressionless Indians wrapped in blankets. The Plaza, always the social and commercial center of life under Spanish and Mexican times, "an open space of mud dirt," remained the marketplace for Indian wares and garden produce. Here the captains and the ricos had their homes, while their servants lived across the river in a little settlement called Analco, an Aztec word meaning "on the other side of the water," clustered around the old chapel of San Miguel. After the arrival of General Kearney, the Americans planted trees and alfalfa in the Plaza and so it remained for many years.

Santa Fe was an old place when the Pilgrims landed at Plymouth. Its land has a charm made up of the customs of four cultures—Indian, Mexican, Spanish, and Anglo. This mixture of four peoples living upon a magnificent land is this State's greatest attraction. There were Indians who lived in places where no Anglo or Spaniard ever has. Before the Pueblo Indians developed their culture in the great river valleys of the State, there were people living in the canyon and mesa country, on the table-lands above the valleys and under the great peaks . . . land that is dry and now deserted by man.

But let us go back a few years and examine some of the early recordings of the features and history of the Palace.

The following is the report to Governor Felix Martinez on the condition in which the Palace of the Governors at Santa Fe was turned over to him in A.D. 1716, by his predecessor, General Juan Ignacio Flores Mogollon.

They ordered Juan de Medina, Miguel Duran and Andres Gonzales, master masons, to examine the said Palacio Real, the shape and size of its rooms and walls, and having done this, they reported that it was all falling down, and (had it not been) for nine buttresses, which had supported it from ancient times on one side and the other, it would have fallen; that only one lofty hall and chamber remain (in condition) together with a room that served as a Chapel where the soldiers recited the rosary of the Blessed Virgin, which Chapel fronts on the Plaza of the Villa; these apartments alone can be used, because all the other rooms and the foundations are falling, as has been said, but the buttresses aforesaid hold up the outside walls, and nearly all the roofs, with their dove-cotes, and the wooden rafters.

Said Palace has a court on the East side, with very dilapidated walls. The main entrances to the Palace are on the South side, on the Royal Palace; through one of them runs a wide covered passageway, giving admittance to the courtyard, where the bodyguard is stationed, and the other court yard serves for the quarters. In said court yard is a stable with a coach-house for the light gig, and two rooms, one above and one below, built of adobe, in which the said General Don Juan Flores kept and used a large chopping-block; and there is a dove-cote where a small lantern used to hang, but nowhere is there any other article in which to grind corn.

At the corners of the Palacio Real stand two towers extremely dilapidated, all of adobe, one of them with seven timbers (props) which hold up the roof, and in that one is now kept the store of gunpowder. The said Governor, Don Felix Martinez, put in a new door as soon as he took possession, realizing that the aforesaid tower ran a great risk, being filled with powder, since its door was broken, and it was easy to enter it. He also had a well dug in the patio, four varas wide and forty varas deep, with a curb of earth and stone, which is partly destroyed. At present it has no water, but there is a wooden bucket. Also said General found in the Palacio Real and took possession of five broken wooden benches made of pine, falling to pieces, six chairs of the same shape, two plain bedsteads with pine slats, and a copper kettle, burned and battered.

The above comprises all the furnishings the said General Don Juan Ignacio Flores found in the Palacio Real, with ten keys to the apartments and chambers; and in official proof thereof we submit the present statement, by virtue of the request of the said Governor and Captain-General, Don Felix Martinez, and which we sign, together with the Secretary of the Calbildo, and seal it with the seal of the Arms of the Kingdom.

Done at the Villa of Santa Fe, New Mexico, on the thirteenth day of the month of July seventeen hundred and sixteen, and on this ordinary paper because no stamped paper is to be had in these parts. Juan Garcia de las Rivas; Francisco Lorenzo de Cassados; Salvador de Montoya.

By order of the Cabildo:

Juan Manuel Chirinos.

Secretary of the Cabildo.

(The above from New Mexico Archive, No. 253. As translated by Ralph Emerson Twitchell.)

"The post and corbel I uncovered in my restoration of the Palace from 1909-13 in the north wall of the Palace in 1910, when it was necessary to rebuild the north wall of the former Ben Hur or Rito de los Frijoles room, might have been the rear area of the passageway of 1716, of which General Juan Ignacio Flores writes."
— Jess Nusbaum.

In a letter to General James Wilkinson, Chihuahua, Mexico, April 20, 1807, Major Zebulon M. Pike, Wilkinson's subordinate officer, explains his entry into Mexican Territory, finding himself and party at the head branches of the Rio del Norte, not far from Taos. They are intercepted by two officers of the Mexican Army, Don Ignacio Saltelo and Don Bartholomew Fernandez, and one hundred soldiers, and proceed to Santa Fe on orders of his excellency Governor Allencaster. Conceiving it proper to comply with this demand, Pike with a number of his party proceed to Santa Fe under guard.

On the afternoon of March 3, 1807 Major Zebulon Montgomery Pike and his remaining group of men spied a haphazard collection of low, flat-roofed houses constructed out of adobe clay—Santa Fe! To Pike it looked like a "fleet of flat-bottomed boats." The town was narrow and long. Its center was a large plaza. Around the sides of this plaza, several one-story tan buildings stood shoulder to shoulder. Most were government offices, but there were also an inn, a few stores and some private residences. The doors were all low, the windows all tiny. Some of the glassless openings were protected by iron bars. A few were equipped with tiny sheets of translucent mica (talc lights) to hold out wind and let in sunlight. Across their fronts stretched wooden awnings supported by posts.

A few narrow streets opened off the plaza and wandered without plan toward the outlying houses. The buildings stood in clusters, surrounded by small fields. There the inhabitants grew grain for making their own bread and the mush they stirred into boiling water and called atole. Plows were mere forked sticks capped with iron. The only vehicles Pike could see were two-wheeled carts pulled by oxen. The sides of the carts were made from woven sticks, so that they looked like overgrown bird cages. Their wheels were solid pieces of wood sawed off the end of a tree trunk. Ungreased, they emitted piercing shrieks as they rolled heavily along the rough roads. There were only horses and donkeys. The broad, black-eyed faces of most of the humbler folk showed a strong mixture of Indian blood.

Halting on the north side of the plaza, the commander of the Spanish troops cleared a path through the crowd and led Pike into a long, low building. This, the guide said, was the Palace of the Governors. Its magnificence, the American could not help thinking, fell short of its title. The roof consisted of layers of poles covered with sod, the floors were hard packed earth. For rugs there were skins of bear, buffalo and mountain lion. Strips of muslin cloth on the walls kept the whitewash from brushing off on the clothing of persons who chanced to touch them. Mingled oddly with these humble furnishings were candlesticks of solid silver and a few pieces of massive carved furniture, evidently imported with great effort from distant Mexico.

In his meeting with the Governor in his "Pike's Tour of New Spain" (*Southwest on The Turquoise Trail*, pp. 225-227. Vol.11) Pike states: "I was wearing a pair of blue trousers, moccasins, blanket coat and a cape made of scarlet cloth, lined with fox skins and my poor fellows in leggings, breech cloths and leather coats and not a hat in the whole party. This appearance was extremely mortifying to us all, especially as soldiers, and although some of the officers were used to frequently observe, 'worth made the man.'

"The governor received me with great austerity at first, and entered into an examination of my business and took possession of all my papers. After all this was explained, he ordered me to a room where officers were confined and a non-commissioned officer to attend me. This being so different from what I had been taught to expect, that I demanded of governor Allencaster, in a written communication, to know if I was to consider myself and party as prisoners of war? He replied in the negative, but ordered to march with my party under protection of Lieutenant Don Facundo Malgares and sixty five of his men and report to General Salcedo at Chihuahua. I was supplied with provisions from the governor's table, and he promised to write to Babtiste La Lande to come down and answer to claims I had against him. The governor's manners and dress were as rich and refined as the candlesticks."

(The above from *The Trail to Santa Fe*, Geo. Lavender, pp. 36-41.)

A civilian doctor, John Robinson, a mysterious fellow, accompanied Pike's group (and then disappears into history) supposedly at the request of a merchant who had hired the aforementioned La Lande to take some trade goods among the Plains Indians. La Lande had vanished. The merchant wanted to recover his losses and when he heard of Pike's expedition, had asked Robinson to accompany the troops as far as the border of New Mexico. From here Robinson planned to reach Santa Fe. On the way he could use his eyes.

The following day Pike and his party left Santa Fe for Chihuahua, and Pike had this to say of the ladies of Santa Fe: "I had caused my men to secrete my papers about their bodies, conceiving it safer than in the baggage; but in the evening, finding the ladies of Santa Fe were treating them to wine, etc. I was apprehensive their interperance might discover (expose) the secret, and took them from all but one (who had my Journal in full) who could not be found, and put them in my trunk . . . but next morning . . . an officer came to take my trunk . . . . Thus my journals were saved at Santa Fe."

At Chihuahua, General Salcedo retained a portion of Pike's papers and conducted an inquisition about them. Eventually Pike and his party were set free. Six years later Pike was killed fighting the British at Toronto in the War of 1812. His report to Washington was released in which Pike expressed the possibility of trade with Santa Fe. By 1815-17, a lucrative commerce with Santa Fe existed; the trade of the prairies had begun in earnest.

There is no evidence that prior to this time the Palace enjoyed any degree of opulence, any more than the personal tastes or wealth of possessions the successive representatives of Mexico, Spain or Pueblos could muster.

In 1803 the United States purchased the Louisiana Territory from France. In 1804, Lewis and Clark were sent across Louisiana's northern reaches to the Pacific Ocean. Mountainmen like Hugh Glenn, Jacob Fowler, the McKnight brothers John and Robert, William Becknell, Samuel Chambers and James Baird, were well-known among the wagon trains.

In one of the caravans in 1826 was a sixteen-year-old named Kit Carson, running away from a saddlemaker to whom he was apprenticed. He became the famous scout, trapper and Indian fighter.

In 1829, Charles and William Bent, the Waldo brothers, and the Frenchman Ceran St. Vrain began the "Bent-St. Vrain Trading Co." in the pioneer town of Franklin, Kansas. Franklin was at that time the general rendevous for the wagons and outfitting place for the commerce of the prairies. Bent-St. Vrain ran stores and traded in Santa Fe and Taos. By May 1831, Independence and Council Grove were gathering places for traders assembling their caravans. They found oxen far superior to mules for fording the rivers with placid skill. The Arkansas River now joined the Ohio and Mississippi rivers as main highways in the push westward.

The Comanches, Pawnees, and Apaches were still dreaded in 1831, when William Wolfskill, a trapper, found a way to avoid the tremendous red gorges that ran into the Grand Canyon of the Colorado. He skirted the high mountains west of the present Zion National Park, then crossed the lower reaches of Nevada and pushed thirstily on across the Mohave to the green valleys of the coast. However, this route could not be used by wagons, and only humble Mexican mule drivers could be called arrieros.

Meanwhile, at the Palace in Santa Fe, Colonel Francisco Perea writes in his 1837-38 narrative of the winter he spent in Santa Fe,

> The Garrita at Santa Fe was a very ordinary structure when compared with the three buildings [Chihuahua, Aquas Calientas, and Monte Rey. —R.N.] I saw while traveling in the interior of Mexico. It was built of sun-dried bricks, laid in clay mortar and without foundations except for perhaps a few stones. Out of use from the time of the American occupation. We found Santa Fe full of soldiers, citizens and a miscellaneous gathering of humanity of all stations of life. The plaza was crowded with all kinds of vehicles, teamsters, roustabouts, horses, mules, burros, pigs and goats. Some were about their campfires preparing food, while others were feeding and caring for their animals. Near the northeast corner of the plaza, which was then surrounded on its four sides by flat-roofed, one-story buildings with portales (porches) in front of them. There were three cottonwood trees of the mountain variety and opposite the Palace stood a flagstaff (pirome), from the top of which hung the Mexican flag in all its glory. The four entrances at the corners of the square were guarded, each with a single cannon of small caliber. The square was dirty, an unsightly place to a degree unbelieveable.

> Hotels in the winter of 1837-38, were all of a most primitive kind, where travelers and others could obtain meals and lodging. Chili was a favored dish and a native wine (vino del pais) was served at table if desired. Fireplaces built into the adobe walls were used for both heating and cooking purposes, there being no stoves of any sort, and fused mica was used as window glazing. There were more dance halls (salas de baile) than Churches and not wanting patronage.

Up at the Garita, Mexican officials continued to collect excessive and varied fees for permits to sell and trade the materials and goods coming into Santa Fe, from the trails, on heavily laden wagons and carts. Further, the corral located just below the Garita, where the trail animals having brought in the goods for "The Santa Fe Trade" were pastured, for which further tribute was extracted, was simply known as SHITTI CORRAL.

At a later time Edgar L. Hewett appeared at a City Council meeting in Santa Fe, asking that these names be changed. He was refused with the saying, "All the odor and romance of years must remain."

14

Following General Armijo's suppression of the insurrection, all customs duties (derechos de arancel), were principally collected from merchandise imported from the United States to the Territory over the Santa Fe Trail and the custom-house was moved to a more central area in the Plaza, where storage was made available and Armijo, himself "jefe" at this port of entry, was extracting as much as $500 per wagon. Many trade groups took to doubling goods on the wagons on the outskirts of the city to escape the excessive taxes Armijo imposed.

In 1820 Mexico gained her independence from Spain, and a more tolerable attitude developed toward the United States. This new friendliness reached northward into New Mexico. The change stimulated commerce, and Santa Fe became the center of trade beyond the western banks of the Mississippi, a link in the chain of communications to the west coast. The war between the United States and Mexico had caused a good deal of concern and President James K. Polk prevailed upon James Magoffin, who for many years had traded and served as vice council in Chihuahua and Durango, to try to convince Governor Manuel Armijo of New Mexico to yield to American occupation.

Magoffin's proposal had been well received but when news reached Santa Fe that an army was being equipped in Missouri to attack Santa Fe, feeling ran high. Armijo issued a proclamation calling on the people to defend their homes and land. His army, made up of inexperienced volunteers, was demoralized. One of his staunchest supporters, La Dona Tules Barcelo, proprietress of "en casa de juego," had turned against him and was supporting the Americans. Armijo called a council of war with his officers and they decided to capitulate and retire to the south.

U.S. General Stephen W. Kearney ordered an emissary, Captain Philip St. George Cooke, to meet with Armijo at the Palace (1846). Cooke describes his meeting: "I entered from the hall, a large and lofty apartment, with a carpeted earth floor . . . the Governor was seated at a table, with six or eight military and civil officials standing. There was no mistaking the Governor, a large and fine looking man, wearing a blue frock coat of sky blue, with a high collar and a General's shoulder straps, his blue trousers trimmed with gold lace, and a red sash. He rose when I was presented to him; I said I was sent to him by the general commanding the American Army, and handed him a letter, as he wished and for his convenience."

Kearney, Commander of the Union forces, had followed the "trace" (Santa Fe Trail) over the Raton Pass and on down to Las Vegas. There on the roof of one of the flat-topped houses on the old town plaza, he addressed the silent crowd. Henceforth, he told them, they were citizens of the United States. Then he marched toward Santa Fe. His scouts told him he might encounter resistance at Glorieta Pass, but this failed to materialize.

On August 18, 1846, Kearney with his volunteer army of seventeen thousand men, of traders, freighters, cavalry and infantry took Santa Fe without a shot. At the Palace, Kearney was received by Governor Juan Bautista y Alarid. "The General talked to the Mexicans in a conversational manner, and his remarks were similar in content to the address he had previously delivered in Las Vegas . . . . When Kearney had finished, Vigil treated his guests to wine and brandy. At this time, and as the sun was setting, the Stars and Stripes were raised over El Palacio, then 236 years old. A salute of thirteen guns were fired by the artillery; that night Kearney slept on the carpeted floor of the Palace of the Governors and his weary troops lay down to rest in their tents on the outskirts of Santa Fe. A low stone marker on the plaza commemorates this date and event."

George Rutledge Gibson, who wrote the above in his *Journal of a Soldier under Kearney and Doniphan, 1846-1847*, continues: "The General was in fine spirits; he took us through the Palace, and introduced us to the ballroom, as well as the large chamber of the Governor's lady. The ballroom is a large, long room, with a dirt floor, and the panels of the interior doors made of bull and buffalo hides, tanned and painted so as to resemble wood. There are various other rooms beside the antechamber, which has the lady's private apartment at one end and the ballroom immediately behind this and parallel to it. The office of Secretary of State is on the east side, and the guard room and prison on the west end of the block. The rear contains kitchens, bake-ovens, and a garden, the whole being roomy, convenient and suitable to the dignity of a Governor of New Mexico. . . . Many parts of the building are in a state of decay and have been neglected for some time, especially the apartments near the calabozo. The walls are all thick, and it contains as few doors and windows as possible."

Ten days later, on August 28, 1846, Kearney held a ball at the Palace. It was a new thing for plain Republicans to revel in a Palace. The rooms were elaborately decorated with the flags of the army. The party commenced assembling about nine o'clock, and dancing soon followed. The General and staff and some of the officers belonging to the regular army were conspicuous in their dress. The crowd was great—at least four or five hundred.

Years later (1954) the author and Jess paid a visit to Lemitar, New Mexico where Armijo had lived after his return from Mexico. We located the old trace, set from west to east toward the river of the 1840's. Here at the end of the old road we located the deteriorated remnants of Armijo's hacienda, and somewhat to the east the old ford over the river in earlier times and the area where a ferry was used to cross the Rio in high water. The original structure had obviously been a small replica of the Palace complex in Santa Fe, minus the south portal. A huge gate had stood on the east, for quick defense and entrance of horses and wagons. What remained of the hacienda was being used as an animal house and for chickens. The lovely blue color could yet be seen in the few nichos in the walls, and the ceilings bore the lovely herringbone design of small, slender aspen trunks.

Our journey took us to Socorro, six miles south, where we were unsuccessful in our efforts to locate the huge and ornate bed which Armijo had brought up from Mexico and used at the Palace. It had been legend at the time Jess was restoring the Palace, 1909-13. We had hoped to return it to the Palace, but were reminded of the close relationship and importance of this area to the history of Santa Fe. Here Coronado had camped in 1541 with 30 of his men, and in May 1598 Oñate, who reconquered New Mexico for Spain, was hospitably received and given a supply of much needed corn.

In recognition for this friendly reception and welcome aid, the Spanish conquistador named this settlement Socorro (succor), in honor of Nuestra Senora del Socorro—later applied to the present Socorro by Friar Alonzo de Benavides, under whose direction the Franciscan Mission was erected in 1628.

It is well to recall this passage from Pedro Vial's Santa Fe-St. Louis diary:

As we now turn to look Southwest on the Turquoise Trail, which became the historic Santa Fe route to puebloland, we essay the study of finding and opening of a great thoroughfare which, although in part laid out on the buffalo routes, ran crosswise, as a rule, to the north-and-south migrations of those shaggy armies of trail-breakers. To them the enterprising settlements of White men at St. Louis, Franklin and Independence to the northeast, and the quaint adobe towns of Taos and Santa Fe under the turquoise skies of the Southern Rockies, meant nothing. Lacking then a known reason for a track between these later centers of population when the West was in "a state of Nature," we assume that the Santa Fe Trail came into existence along with the White man's need for it, in the days of which Stoddard, Houck, Bloom and Bolton have written, when traders "to the Mexican mountains" fared forth from the Mississippi and the Spanish governors at Santa Fe desired to open communications with Spain's other "outposts of Empire" on the "Father of Waters."

(The above from *Southwest on the Turquoise Trail*, Vol. II, p. 43.)

We learn of Vial's task in this new land through a letter from the Governor of Santa Fe to the Commandant at St. Louis:

Pedro Vial, who is appointed by order of His Excellency, the Viceroy of Nueva Espana, to open communications in this province which is under my (Don Fernando de la Concha, Governor of Santa Fe) charge, between it and the other settlements which the King possesses in this America, sets out on this date May 21, 1792 with the design of opening communications with respect to Los Ylinneses (Illinois), which is a dependency of the government of Louisiana.

(The above from same vol., pp. 44-45, Vial's Santa Fe-St. Louis Diary.)

Vial did not "break the path" of the later Santa Fe Trail precisely, but he did establish a communication and left the first "Santa Fe Trail Diary."

Captain Thomas Becknell, whose *Journal of 1821* will always remain a classic of the plains, wrote, as recorded in *Southwest on the Turquoise Trail,*

On Tuesday morning of the 13th, we had the satisfaction of meeting with a party of Spanish troops. Although the difference in our language would not admit to conversation, yet the circumstances attending their reception of us, fully convinced us of their hospitable disposition and friendly feelings. Being likewise in a strange country, and subject to their disposition, our wishes lent their aid to increase our confidence in their manifestations of kindness. The discipline of the officers was strict, and the subjection of the men appeared almost servile. We encamped with them that night, and the next day about 1 o'clock, arrived at San Michael [San Miguel] the conduct of whose inhabitants gave us greatful evidence of civility and welcome. Fortunately I here met with a Frenchman, whose language I perfectly understood, and hired him to proceed with us to Santa Fe, in the capacity of interpreter. We left here early in the morning. During the day passed another village named St. Baw (Pecos ruins), and the remains of an ancient fortification, supposed to have been constructed by the aboriginal Mexican Indians. The next day, after crossing a mountain country, we arrived at Santa Fe and were received with apparent pleasure and joy. It is situated in a valley of the mountains, on a branch of the Rio del Norte or North River, and some twenty miles from it. It is the seat of Government of the province; is about two miles long and one mile wide, and compactly settled. The day of my arrival I accepted an invitation to visit the Governor, whom I found to be well informed and gentlemanly in manners; his demeanor was courteous and friendly. He asked many questions concerning my country, its people, their manner of living, etc.; expressed a desire that the Americans would keep up an intercourse with that country, and said that if any of them wished to emigrate, it would give him pleasure to afford them every facility.

The people are generally swarthy, and live in a state of extreme indolence and ignorance. Their mechanical improvements are very limited, and they appear to know little of the benefit of industry, or the advantage of the arts. Corn, rice and wheat are their principal productions; they have very few garden vegetables, except the onion, which grows large and abundantly; the seeds are planted nearly a foot apart, and produce onions from four to six inches in diameter. Their atmosphere is remarkably dry, and rain is uncommon except in the months of July and August. To remedy this inconvenience, they substitute with tolerable advantage, the numerous streams which descend from the mountains by damming them up, and conveying the water over their farms in ditches. Their domestic animals consist chiefly of sheep, goats, mules and asses.

Like the French they live in villages; the rich keep the poor in dependence and subjection. Laborers are hired for about three dollars per month; their general employment is that of herdsmen, and to guard their flocks from a nation of Indians called Navahoes, who sometimes murder the guards and drive away their mules and sheep. The circumstance of their farms begin wholly unfenced, obliges them to keep their stock some distance from home. The walls of their houses are two or three feet thick, built of sun-dried brick, and are uniformly one story high, having a flat roof made of clay, and the floors are made of the same material. They do not know the use of plank and have neither chairs nor tables although the rich have rough imitation of our settee, which answers the treble purpose of chair, table and bedstead.

Marmaduke, in his journal of 1824, writes:

Arrived at Santa Fe about dusk. This is quite a populous place, but is built entirely of mud houses; some parts of the city are tolerably regularly built, others very irregular. The inhabitants appear to be friendly, and some of them are very wealthy; but by far the greater part are the most miserable, wretched, poor creatures that I have ever seen; yet they appear to be quite happy and contented in their miserable priest-ridden situation. The city is well supplied with good water; provisions very scarce; a great many beggars seen to be walking the streets. The distance from Franklin, Mo. to this place is estimated at 931 miles. Entered our goods and arranged our taxes with the collector who appears to be an astonishingly obliging man as a public officer. Remained in town and endeavored to sell goods, which we found difficult to do to advantage owing to the scarcity of money and the quality of the goods.

(The above paragraph from *Southwest on the Turquoise Trail*, p. 75.)

In 1847, William Bent decided to go to Taos for a few days of rest with his Mexican wife Ignacia and their three children. At the time Kit Carson's wife Josefa was staying with them. Bent knew there were no troops in Taos. At dawn on

January 19, a howling mob of Mexican and Indian supporters came to the house. He stepped outside and an arrow killed him. His family was left unharmed but many Americans were killed. One named Charles Towne escaped and made his way 70 miles to Santa Fe to report the uprising to Kearney, who assembled St. Vrain and over fifteen hundred Mexicans went up. The rebels fortified themselves in the windowless church at the Pueblo. Cannon were brought up and they were defeated with holes blasted into the walls of the church. William had been the survivor of the four Bent brothers. Robert had been killed by the Comanches. Charles died at Taos and George had been taken ill and died at Bent's fort.

On the trails, the Delawares were being hired as hunters to the wagons and the Plains Indians—Pawnees, Comanches, Kiowas, Utes and Apaches—were on the move. Indians who "buried" their dead by placing them on platforms in high branches of trees found the traders quick to rob the graves of curios. These groves of trees served the Indians for shade in summer and shelter in winter and many a pony survived on their bark. Traders cut them and often left enough smoldering fire to have kept a tepee warm for a week. Indians themselves shot buffalo to trade hides for alcohol, guns and ammunition. Taos was still a tiny New Mexico village of flat-roofed adobe houses some seventy miles north of Santa Fe. Raton Pass was almost impassable for wagons and difficult until 1876, when a fellow disguised as a sheepherder surveyed a route over the Raton Pass to Trinidad for the Santa Fe Railway Co. He was Raymond Morley. He was joined by Uncle Dick Wootton, the trapper, and the first train went over the pass in January, 1879.

There had been much confusion and considerable activity at the Palace of the Governors during the Civil War. The Confederates planned to invade New Mexico to hijack California's overland gold shipments eastward and take over the silver and gold mines of Colorado.

To the west of Santa Fe and under protection can yet be seen the tracks of camels introduced into the Southwest by Edward Fitzgerald Beale (1822-1893), who was well acquainted with the West. He was a junior officer of the U.S. frigate "Congress" when it reached Monterey in 1846 and under Robert F. Stockton took part in the annexation of California, and was with the detachment that reached General Kearney just before Kearney's forces were surrounded by the Mexicans in the battle of San Pasqual. With Kit Carson, Beale made his way through enemy lines to summon Stockton's aid. He and Carson were sent overland to Washington with dispatches and while crossing the desert he conceived the idea of using camels for transportation. He persuaded Jefferson Davis, then Secretary of War, to import camels and he used them in his 1857 survey of a wagon road from Fort Defiance to the Colorado River. His report contains a most interesting glimpse of Santa Fe:

"August 12, 1857. Started my train on, it being necessary for me to remain until the arrival of the express from Santa Fe. I was anxious moreover, to get the men out of town as soon as possible, as the fandangos and other pleasures had rendered them rather troublesome. This morning I was obliged to administer a co- pious supply of oil to boot to several, especially to my Turks and Greeks with the camels. The former had not found a sufficient reason for temperance, but was as drunk as any Christian in the train, and would have remained behind, but for a style of reason much resorted to by the head of his church."

In 1776 when Escalante left Santa Fe, to find a way to Monterey, California, the Casas Reales was a defensive post. Looking back to Pike's visit to Santa Fe, an enormous energy developed on the American Continent.

General Henry H. Sibley had been a former major at Fort Union and had changed his allegiance. Leading the Confederates one hundred miles to the north he had taken Albuquerque, and on March 16th Santa Fe fell to his forces. The Confederate banner flew over the Palace of the Governors and here Sibley planned his assault on the early log-built, shabby, vulnerable Fort Union of the late 1850's. Sibley continued at the Palace until his defeat in the skirmish at Apache Canyon, New Mexico, March 26, 1862.

In 1870, Governor William A. Pile, tired of the mounds of accumulated records and possibly unaware of history's meaning, sold as scrap paper the records which had been accumulating at the Palace since 1693.

With the coming of the railways, William H. Jackson, the noted photographer, wrote:

> The Union Pacific and the Central Pacific—the one from the east, the other from the west—were intent on winning as much of the route for themselves as possible. In 1868 the Central Pacific had crossed the Sierras and was rushing its construction eastward over the Nevada deserts, while the Union Pacific was crowding its forces across mountainous Wyoming in a desperate effort to reach the valley of the Great Salt Lake before the Central got to this objective.

In 1869, while photographing along the railroad, Jackson first met the noted geologist Dr. F.V. Hayden, then conducting what was officially known as the United States Geological Survey of the Territories. Jackson joined the Hayden Survey of 1870, which covered southern Wyoming with a staff of some twenty men. The expedition supplies were transported in four wagons, each drawn by a four-mule team. When on the march, the men, all mounted, roamed widely as did Jackson in pursuit of their assignments and returned to the wagons only at the end of the day when camp had been made.

In his noted *Westward America*, Howard R. Driggs graphically describes the year 1851:

> I stood on an eminence overlooking this valley, grassy and a mile wide and straight for many miles, level as a floor, bare of any trees or brush, and on each side bluffs stretching away east and west a parallel of lines to the horizon. From bluff to bluff on the north and south and up the valley to the westward—as far as the eye could reach—the broad valley was literally blackened by a compact mass of buffalo; and not only this—the massive bluffs on both sides were covered by thousands of thousands and thousands that were pouring down into the already crowded valley . . . the living dark masses covered the ground completely as a carpet covers the floor (p. 61).

The greed of professional buffalo hunters which followed the bloody struggle between soldiers and the redmen all but completely exterminated the animals. After the Civil War, as the railroads began to penetrate the regions where the bison still roamed in great numbers, bands of these hunters, armed with repeating rifles, went out to slay. Their object was to get hides, each of which sold for three dollars or less. As a result of this slaughter, the plains were soon covered with skinned carcasses. Some idea of the extent of this destruction of big game may be had from records of shipment of the brown pelts on the railroad. At one time fifty thousand of them were piled in the freight yards in Dodge City, Kansas.

Albert Pike wrote in his *Narrative of a Journey in the Prairie – 1831*: "Neither is the Governor's Palace in Santa Fe anything more than a mud building, fifteen feet high with a mud covered portico, supported by rough pine pillars." (*Publication of the Arkansas Historical Society*, Vol. 4, p. 98.) Nor seemingly had Santa Fe changed very much when in 1846 (the Palace having just become the property of the United States Government) Lt. Col. Edwin Vose Sumner took command at Fort Marcy, on the hilltop 600 yards above the Palace, and wrote that he considered the Capital City a "sink of vice and extravagance" as he marched his troops eastward, away from the evils of Santa Fe's faro, fandangos and "Taos lightning" into the "boondocks on the Mora." There they built the first fort named "Union" to the tune as they sang: "There's a land that is fairer than this and we'll reach it bye and bye."

A period followed when the Palace undoubtedly underwent changes and repairs of a sort, but a letter of interest comes to our attention, written on December 21, 1851 by Judge Grafton Baker, then chief justice of the New Mexico Supreme Court, to Daniel Webster, then Secretary of State: "We enter the plaza at the northeast corner, and immediately the eye ranges along the portal of the palace in front of which we are now standing. It is not far, from three hundred and fifty feet in length, and varies from twenty to seventy five feet in width." (Baker to Webster: National Archives, Misc. Letters, Dept. of State.)

The best of the early accounts comes to us from W.W.H. Davis, who was appointed United States Attorney in 1853 and who printed a book in 1857, based upon the diaries of his New Mexico experiences, called *El Gringo or New Mexico and Her People*:

> I would beg leave to call attention to the necessity of providing temporarily, rooms suitable for the accommodation of the Supreme Court of the Territory. The terms of the Supreme Court are fixed at Santa Fe, and the same rooms might serve for the accommodation of the District Court of the First Judicial District, and the Circuit Court of Santa Fe County. There is at the northeast corner of the Plaza, a building containing one large room, (70 x 26 feet) and several smaller ones well suited for the use of juries, Marshal and Clerk, which may with the expenditure of a few hundred dollars to make the necessary adaptations, be made to answer very well for the purposes of the several courts located in Santa Fe. This building, as I have been informed, had always, prior to the conquest of the country by our armies, been used and occupied by the civil authorities of the Province of New Mexico for civil purposes—it has been held and, until recently, occupied by the military authorities of the Territory (p. 168).

Once again repairs on the Old Palace had become an urgent necessity when H.H. Heath, then Secretary of the Territory reported on August 20, 1867 on the condition of the Palace:

> The Palace, as it is familiarly known, is an ancient adobe building; its walls are from 2 to 3½ feet in thickness, which, considering its great

age, remain in remarkably good and sound condition, with some exceptions. From time to time, evidently, judging from appearances since the erection of the main building, additions have been made and probably some new walls inserted. At present, however, with the exception of the west end which was improved last year, under authority from the Secretary of the Treasury which was then as it is now, used for a public depository, the whole building may be said to be in great general dilapidation, a few repairs having been made upon it since becoming the property of the Government . . . . Under authority of the Treasury, recently obtained, the inconsiderable sum of $5000 is now being expended in general repair upon the building and for making such special alterations therein as will inure to its preservation. These improvements however, contemplate no material internal or external architectural changes in the Palace, etc. They propose however, among other things the removal of the territorial library to a large and somewhat more suitable room, the substitution of a stable which adjoins the building for a legislative council chamber, and the room in which the library now is, in the east end of the building, to be taken for the legislature, may, when the legislature is not in session, be used for the federal courts of the Territory.

The H.H. Heath and Henry S. Martin diagrams regarding the changes are in conflict, but with knowledge of the primitive conditions that existed in that period we can with some accuracy follow again the descriptions of General Davis as carried in *El Gringo*, to which we now return:

The first apartments we came to in the rounds of the palace are the office of the secretary of the Territory, which we enter through a quaint little old-fashioned door. The office is divided into two rooms: an inner one, in which the books and records are kept, and where the secretary transacts his official business, and an outer one, used as an anti-room and a store room. The latter is divided by a cotton curtain, hanging down from the beams above, into two compartments, one of which is stored with the old manuscripts and records of the Territory which have been accumulating for nearly three hundred years. The stranger will be struck with the primitive appearance of these ruins: the roof supported by a layer of great pine beams, blackened and stained by age; the floors are earthen, and the woodwork is heavy and rough, and in the style of two centuries ago. [Beams such as Nusbaum found, according to his records in 1909-13.]

On Dec. 2, 1873, the Santa Fe *New Mexican* printed the following:

In a little over one week the legislature of New Mexico will meet in Santa Fe, and it is quite interesting to see all the filth of the Plaza and the surrounding streets gathered into one vast pile in front of the "Palace" where it is more conspicuous than elsewhere. This pile of filth with the papers and loose stuff is blown all through the entire length of the portal of the "Palace," and this mixed with the deposits of the burros, who are daily permitted to use this portal for a stable, is fast causing a very savory smell for those who will soon assemble to make laws for this Territory. By what authority, the filth of the city is piled up in the most public place in the Territory we have not yet learned.

The same issue of the paper continues:

> The Thanksgiving party at the Governor's Palace last night was one of the grandest ever given in Santa Fe. The house was filled with guests: indeed, it seemed as if the whole city was there. During the whole evening Governor and Mrs. Giddings moved from place to place attending to the wants and adding to the enjoyment of the guests.

The weekly *New Mexican* of December 9, 1873 reports:

> The astonishment of the legislators knew no bounds when, instead of entering the dingy mud holes of two years ago, they found themselves surrounded with clean white walls and ceilings; with paint and graining; with new desks and easy chairs; with cleanliness, neatness, light and comfort .... It is sufficient to say that both the House and Senate halls have been thoroughly repaired; ceilings put on; walls plastered; windows, doors, desks, wood boxes, etc., made, painted and grained; and the library hall fitted up for committee rooms.

Reporting on the frontage of the Palace in 1877, the *New Mexican* declared:

> The frontage of the Palace ... now looks as speckled and spotted as Joseph's coat or Dave Montgomery's statuary. U.S. Marshal, John E. Sherman, is just having completed his fine office on the western corner, formerly the U.S. Depository. He has had a low stone wall run along the end of the building to protect the foundation; a plank sidewalk has been placed in front; the wooden pillars supporting the portal roof have been faced, capped with heavy moulding and stone bases placed under them; this with the ornate cornice in the front, adds very much to the appearance of that end of the Palace. With Marshal Sherman is a lawyer E.A. Fiske; next to Governor S.F. Axtell's office and rooms, and Hon. W.F.M. Arny's residence, looking every inch their age, and as if they hadn't been repaired during the ages which have rolled over them. Then comes Attorney General Breeden's office, with granite finish and in good shape; then the territorial library and Senate Chamber, with their frontage in its original condition—naked adobes—on both streets.

We know that in addition James S. Calhoun, who was Indian agent and governor at Santa Fe, made use of a room in the west end of the Palace for Indian affairs. As Davis describes it:

> Opening into the same vestibule (from the Territorial Library) is the office of superintendent of Indian Affairs, which, with a storeroom adjoining, occupies the west end of the Palace building. Nearby is a large vacant room, appropriated to the use of Indians when they come in to see the superintendent on business, at which times they are fed by the government.

(The above from *The Adobe Palace*, p. 12.)

The southwest corner has had an interesting history. At the beginning of the American occupation it was used by the Office of Indian Affairs. It continued to be used for that purpose until 1856, when *El Gringo* was printed. In 1867 it became the public depository and is so shown on the Heath and Martin diagrams. The Ritch plan of 1877 shows the space as "late U.S. depository and still occupied by the receiver of the U.S. Land Office of Santa Fe, New Mexico." The Twitchell ground plan of 1882 shows it as the office of the U.S. Attorney and U.S. Marshal; the Prince rough plan shows it as the residence of the Secretary of the Territory, and in an 1889 diagram, as the U.S. Post Office (as Nusbaum found it being used under Government contract when he began restorations in 1909). In a previous time it had been the office of the Second National Bank of Santa Fe; there was much encroachment for small periods of time by private and city interests.

Nusbaum's notes in this connection state: "It was possibly about 1878 when Territorial Secretary and Acting Governor Ritch prepared designs and plans for construction of the gingerbread portal and balustrade across the front of the Palace of the Governors, and put brick coping across the east end and a brick coping on adobe chimneys, both novelties in the New Mexico period of the time and Ritch said he used his own skills in so doing and carrying out the work. This 2/3 of the portal came under the jurisdiction of the Secretary of the Interior. The west 1/3 came under the Secretary of the Treasury and thereafter a commission of Santa Fe citizens asked the Secretary of the Treasury for funds for a similar modernization of the west end of the portal (Federal end of the building) and to provide a vault for Federal money deposits." This vault was removed by Nusbaum in his stabilization and repair of the Palace 1909-13. He had the Penitentiary completely remove the vault.

But political byplay was still not at an end. According to Davis:

> The postmaster general, T.D. Hour, on January 6, 1883, asked the secretary of the interior, to set aside the old depository space for a post-office, and the following day Henry M. Teller, secretary of the interior, sent instructions to the secretary of the Territory to make the space available to the postmaster. A month later, an inspector from the post office department informed his chief that he had been in Santa Fe waiting for the Second National Bank to move and that the bank moved late Saturday night but failed to keep its agreement to deliver peaceable possession to the department when the bank building was ready to be acquired. D.K. Osborne, a clerk of the Texas, Santa Fe and Northern Railway, headed by T.B. Catron, had jumped the property as a squatter.

(The above from *The Adobe Palace*, pp. 17-19.)

Ritch then gave the background for the "occupation." Osborne had indicated that he would not interfere if the Internal Revenue Office wanted the rooms but that he would not vacate them for the Post Office. Says Ritch, "It has been suggested to me that a solution would be found in the following facts. Osborne is a clerk of a certain railroad company of which T.B. Catron is president. Catron owns the building now occupied by the Santa Fe Post Office and rents said building to the Post Office for a liberal rental. It is important as maintaining a material value of the property thus occupied and that adjoining, also belonging to Mr. Catron, that the post office remain where it is and not be removed as was proposed to the property jumped by the clerk of Mr. Catron's railroad company."

It would hardly be important to tell in detail the rest of the story. George W. Pritchard, who had been made United States attorney for New Mexico, brought suit against Fiske and Warren for the southwest corner room and got judgement against them. Thus began the steady legal process by which Breeden, Dr. Sloan, Fiske, Warren and agents of the T.B. Catron Company were forced from the building.

The letter dated February 6, 1883, from L.F. Lee, inspector, to Col. David B. Parker, chief post office inspector at Washington, reads in part: "Sec. Ritch, when I showed him your dispatch, agreed to give me possession of the premises for the Department yesterday morning. When visiting the building, was surprised to find the clerk of the Texas, Santa Fe and Northern Railway in possession, having moved his furniture in the building during the night. Spiegelberg, President of the Second National Bank, is one of the principal stockholders or the Treasurer of the Railway. Mr. Breeden, council for the jumpers, is Vice President of the bank. It looks to me as though the government had no right here that the old Santa Fe ring was bound to respect. They assert that the building is not Government property and that any squatter or jumper who takes possession can maintain his claim against the Government."

Beginning July 7, 1881, W.G. Ritch, as secretary of the Territory and custodian of public buildings, carried on a long series of differences with then Attorney General Henry M. Breeden. Ritch had written to the Secretary of the Interior on May 27, 1881, informing him that Breeden had entered upon and taken possession of a piece of land "known and heretofore occupied, as the garden lot and being as near as may be the north half of the Adobe Palace property." His letter pointed out that the garden had been cultivated under permission of Governor Lew Wallace since Wallace came to the territory as governor. Ritch claimed that Breeden had taken possession of the lot with the intention "to erect a building thereon for use of the post office." The device used by Breeden and his friends was interesting. They had attempted to enter on the land by use of half-Indian scrip. The General Land Office later held that to be an improper use of the scrip.

It was in this period when Adolph Bandelier arrived to make the first extensive survey of this region between 1880-1886 and scarcely seven months since the completion of the railway to the Capitol. He wrote he slept the first night with bedbugs and of his first day in Santa Fe he wrote: "Houses all adobe, some new. Population 6500. Saw Pueblo Indians on the streets, fine fellows clad in white, with hair tressed and hanging down each side. Driving a herd of burros . . . meat (sheep and beef) hung out on the portales."

General Lew Wallace served as Territorial Governor of New Mexico, and his appointment was with American destiny from 1878-1881. Santa Fe was a hell-raising, rampaging sin spot: mecca of men who wanted liquor, faro, fandangos and women; all raw in the time of William Bonney and his gang of outlaws, Charlie Bowdre, Tom O'Folliard, Doc Skurlock, Fred Wayte, Jim French, John Middleton, Hendry Brown, Tom Cooper, Dave Rudabaugh, Billy Wilson, Tom Webb and others. Billy Bonney as a young boy was smiling and good natured, not handsome but with a certain sort of devil-may-care and unstudied easy deliberate movements. He was forearmed even when not forewarned and forever on guard. A child in years but with a soul out of the frozen Dark Ages; charged with a heritage of sinister sophistication, who would meet any problem as it arose in an instinctive flash, that only murder could solve, and he solved it with murder without a moment's hesitation.

The Kid was not the stuff of ordinary men. Like a sailor he had a sweetheart in every port. In every placita, in the Pecos, some little senorita was proud to be known as his *quirida*. Long after Billy's death at the gun of Patrick Floyd Garrett, one could hear tales of the Kid, for instance while sitting on one of the benches under the shade of old trees in the Plaza, fronting the Palace in Santa Fe, where the rich and poor of this ancient villa came each day to talk of events, sometimes in low tones. Mention Billy the Kid and immediately eyes would light and interminable stories flow. Many a time when the Kid was an outlaw with a price on his head he had ridden into town and danced all night at the dancehall on Galisteo Street. The house, now gone, was of pinkish adobe with a blue door and window shutters. Did the police ever arrest him? Not even when he lived in Santa Fe for a time. Why, the boy wasn't afraid of the devil himself.

Drop by any little adobe in Santa Rosa, or on the Hondo, or Puerta de Luna— anywhere, between the Ratons and Seven Rivers and the Mexican housewife would serve her tortillas and beans with a soft smile on her lips at mention of Billy's name and you would be likely to hear, between your mouthfuls of beans and chili scooped up with one of the torn tortillas: "Billee the Keed? Ah, you have hear of heem? He was one gran'boy, senor. All Mexican pepul his friend. You nevair hear a Mexican say one word against Billee the Keed. Everybody love that boy. He was so kind hearted, so generous. So brave. And so 'andsome. Madre de Dios! Every little senora tried to catch Billee the Keed for their sweetheart. Ah, many little muchacha cry her eyes out when he is keel; and when she counts her beeds at Mass, she add a prayer for good measure for his soul to rest in peace. Poor Billee the Keed; muy valiente, muy caballero."

General Lew Wallace had taken up residence at the Palace of the Governors at Santa Fe in August, 1878, determined to carry out President Hayes' orders to end the Lincoln County feud. Wallace wrote:

> When I reached Santa Fe I found the law was practically a nullity and had no way of asserting itself. The insurrection seemed to be confined to one county which strangely enough was called Lincoln. I received statements of judges that they dared not hold court in certain districts. The United States Marshal told me he had a large number of warrants which he dared not serve and he could not find deputies rash enough to attempt service when they knew their lives would pay the penalty. The military commander at Fort Stanton sent me a list of murders that had been committed in that part of the country. I forwarded these combined statements to President Hayes. (From *The Saga of Billy the Kid*, pp. 150-157.)

Governor Wallace, in his investigation of the Lincoln County situation, acquainted himself with both sides of the story through conferences with Murphy and McSween, who met him in the capital. Mrs. McSween, through her lawyer, George Chapman of Las Vegas, prepared a number of affidavits which she forwarded to the governor, giving the details of the burning of her home, the murder of her husband, and Colonel Dudley's actions while in Lincoln County with his troops. Sheriff Peppin and other Murphy leaders also sent affidavits. Both John Chisum and U.S. Commissioner Angel called on Governor Wallace and endeavoured to give him a clear understanding of the vendetta, its causes, battles, and present status. However, with conflicting statements before him, clear understanding of so complex a problem was difficult.

Governor Wallace had grave doubts from the first as to his ability to end the feud. But that was the specific problem given him by President Hayes to solve and he set himself to the task. His first step was to issue a proclamation of amnesty to all who had taken part in the war, except under indictment for crime, on the understanding that they lay down their arms. This action was to some extent effective. There had practically been no more fighting nor, for that matter, had there been since the big battle in Lincoln; but nothing the Governor could do could terminate the bitter hatreds the war had kindled or prevent the deadly spirit of the feud from smoldering dangerously for years.

Billy the Kid ignored the Governor's proclamation. Since the death of McSween, there was no faction leader to claim his allegiance, and he had moreover acquired the habit of outlawry. He doubtless had no desire for any other mode of life. Since there was no longer any McSween faction exchequer upon which to draw, he and his outlaw gang lived by gambling and the wholesale rustling of livestock, making their rendezvous for the time in the mountains near Fort Stanton.

Governor Wallace determined to have a personal interview with Billy the Kid and use his powers of persuasion to induce him to settle down to a useful citizenship, or perhaps to move elsewhere to make a new start. With this purpose in mind, he drove from Santa Fe to Fort Stanton and on to Lincoln.

Governor Wallace sat with General Hatch, Juan Patron, and a group of army officers on the porch of the Ellis House as a lone horseman appeared riding slowly toward them through Lincoln Street. "Here comes the Kid," remarked Juan Patron. They viewed the picturesque figure of the young outlaw with fixed attention.

The Kid carried a rifle across his saddle-bows, and if the men's eyes had been keen enough, they might have noted that the gun was cocked. The Kid had ridden into Lincoln from the west by the Fort Stanton road and came on at a running walk past the Murphy store, headquarters of his enemies, without so much as turning his head to glance at a group of men lounging there who eyed him with cold hatred. Hitching his horse in front of the Ellis House, he walked briskly up the path to the porch, his rifle in his hand, his six-shooter at his belt. Governor Wallace rose.

"So you are Billy the Kid," asked the Governor of the outlaw.

"I am," said the outlaw to the Governor.

The two men shook hands.

It was a meeting not so much of two men, as of two worlds. They clasped hands across the gulf of ages. One constructive, the other would soon be extinct and pass into history. The Governor showed slight surprise.

"You don't look at all as I had pictured you in mind." The Governor smiled. "Here you are a clean-cut good-looking youth of nineteen. But I had heard stories about you."

The Kid declined the point.

"I am old enough to be your father. So, Billy, I am going to talk to you like a father."

The Kid nodded.

"I have come all this way to Lincoln for the special purpose of persuading you to stop all this fighting. I have faith you can help me. You see, President Hayes has sent me to New Mexico to establish peace. He has the confidence that I will do it. I am going to try to justify his confidence. Therefore, I have issued a proclamation of amnesty to all who have taken part in this feud, and I want you especially to share in it."

"I couldn't if I tried. You don't know this country, Governor. Look up the street. Do you see those men standing at Murphy's store?"

"Yes."

"They're Murphy's men. That's Jimmy Dolan, 'Dad' Peppin, Andy Boyle, old man Pearce. They'd kill me so fast I wouldn't know what happened."

Small talk ensued as the Kid patted his rifle, then thoughtfully lifting it, blew a fleck of dust off the magazine. Abstractedly, his free hand rested on the handle of his ivory six-shooter.

Once again the Governor urged Billy to stand trial on whatever charges might be brought against him and stated, "That would wipe the slate clean. If you are convicted, I give you my promise now that I will pardon you and set you free, but first I want to see you stand trial like a man."

"No jury would acquit me of anything."

Neither spoke for a moment.

"It's the only way to wipe the slate clean, my boy," said the Governor.

"You are wrong in your attitude. But if I can't persuade you to change it, that would seem to end the matter."

They rose and shook hands.

"Goodbye, Governor," said the Kid.

"Goodbye, my boy," said the Governor.

Governor Wallace watched the Kid as he rode off along the canyon road until he disappeared.

"If that boy would take my advice," he said, turning to his companions with a note of sadness in his voice, "I believe he has in him the making of a fine man."

The Kid did not surrender for trial. The pardon did not come, and his friendship turned to hate. "The Lincoln County reign of terror is not over," wrote Mrs. Susan E. Wallace, the governor's wife, in a letter from Fort Stanton, "and we hold our lives at the mercy of desperados and outlaws, chief among them Billy the Kid, whose boast is that he has killed a man for every year of his life. Once he was captured and escaped, and now he swears, when he has killed the sheriff, the judge who passed sentence upon him, and Governor Wallace, he will surrender and be hanged. 'I mean to ride into the plaza at Santa Fe, hitch my horse in front of the Palace, and put a bullet through Lew Wallace.' These were his words. One of my friends warned me to close the shutters at evening, so the bright light of the student lamp might not make such a shining mark of the Governor writing until late upon *Ben Hur*."

Mrs. Wallace's picture of the author sitting by the open window of the Palace working upon his book late into the night under the light of the lamp, with the vague menace of Billy the Kid's six-shooter out in the darkness of Santa Fe's silent streets, adds credence to what Wallace himself has written: "Everybody has heard of the Old Palace at Santa Fe, New Mexico. A rambling one story structure, with walls in places six feet thick and hard as friable stone. It covers the whole of the north side of the Plaza."

There are those who have said Wallace wrote his *Ben Hur* as he paced the south portal facing the Plaza; others swear he wrote the story seated under a tree in the patio of the Palace near the old well, where Spanish treasure is said to have been buried. No doubt he sought the entire area in his imaginative pursuit of the novel and it is an anomaly, perhaps, that it could be written at all in a time and place where anybody could get away with anything he wished, if he had big enough fists, or a trigger finger to support him. Each trod and rode the "trail" for his purposes. For them all the place offered a haven, as Wallace sought to bring in order and at a time when national fortunes were altering, was writing at the Palace:

The second floor from the west end front of the Palace opens into a spacious passage, and does one seek a conference with the governor, he must knock on the first left hand door in the passage . . . . Back of the executive office is an extensive room provided with a small window and one interior entrance, the walls were grimy, the undressed boards of the floor rested flat on the ground, the cedar rafters (vigas) rain-stained and overweighted with tons and tons of mud composing the roof, had the threatening downward curvature of a shipmate's cutlass. Nevertheless, in the cavernous chamber I wrote the eighth and last book of *Ben Hur*. [Nusbaum states that in 1910, he found this was Governor George Curry's office —R.N.] . . . My custom when night came was to lock the door and bolt the windows of the office proper, and with a student's lamp, bury myself in the four soundless walls of the forbidding annex and once there at my rough pine table the Count of Monte Cristo in his dungeon of stone was not more lost to the world . . . . The ghosts if they were about, did not disturb me—yet in the hush of that gloomy harborage, I beheld the Crucifixion, and strove to write what I beheld.

Wallace could not have known the words of the chorus of the "Ballad of Ben Hur" to which the author, in her early years, marched while attending Baraga Convent School at Marquette, Michigan, so very far from the Palace at Santa Fe.

Brave Ben Hur. Prince of his race.
God-like in form. God-like in face.
Skilled and strong. He'll stand the pace,
Till the race is won.

When General Lew Wallace left the Palace, the time was still big with fate in the history of the West. Patrick Floyd Garrett appeared on the scene, a Southerner and an unknown who had no experience in man-hunting. He had no reputation as a fighter as far as a shocked Fort Sumner knew; his only qualifications were his intimate friendship with the Kid and his men. He was familiar with all their old haunts, trails and secret places of rendezvous and refuge.

When Garrett became sheriff the friendship ended. All the forces of law were now marshalled to aid the new sheriff. After a winter of continued depredations, the Kid and three of his men were captured at Arroyo Tivan and landed in the caloboso in Santa Fe. The penitentiary south of town had not been built. If the Kid had suspected this would happen, Garrett would have been dead.

Billy was taken to Mesilla, a little town, predominantly Mexican, on the west bank of the Rio Grande opposite Las Cruces. Here he stood trial for the shooting of sheriff James A. Brady of Lincoln County, before the court of Judge Warren H. Bristol, defended by attorney Ira E. Leonard of Lincoln. The Kid was sentenced to hang.

After a few weeks the Kid accomplished a wily trick against his jailer in a game of "Monte." Deputy Sheriff J.W. Bell of White Oaks lost his gun to Billy and was shot. The Kid then cornered Old Man Goss, the cook, who was ordered to get an axe and chop the chains off the Kid's leg irons.

But the Kid was nearing the end of the trail, and in the rambling old abandoned Officer's Quarters of twenty rooms at Old Fort Sumner that Lucien B. Maxwell and his wife Senorita Luz Beaubien, had made their home, Billy was shot by Pat Garrett, as he visited Pete Maxwell in his bedroom in an attempt to locate Billy. As he was talking with Pete, the unsuspecting Kid walked into the dark room and was shot.

No one can tell that story without telling of the child that Lucien had purchased from a band of wandering Navajo Indians for the sum of fifty dollars. The girl took the name of Deluvina Maxwell and served the family for many years. In return for a favor the Kid had given Deluvina the only photo of himself that he carried and she idolized him all the days of her life. No one could weave the spell of the woman who had been Billy's only true love as could Paulita Maxwell Jaramillo.

After the Kid's death, Pat Garrett left a legend of devotion to the law, but as fate would have it, his own end came by the gun of Wayne Brazel, a cattleman, over a dispute about a land lease to Brazel. Governor George Curry, the last Territorial Governor to reside at the Palace in Santa Fe, was one of the pallbearers.

The tellers of tall stories can still be found in the plaza at Santa Fe, sitting under the trees as of old. Perhaps even now one of them will point to the south of the Plaza and tell how long ago, in 1760, Governor Francisco Marin del Valle started the military chapel, "La Castrense," and how from 1827 to 1846, General Manuel Armijo, who served three terms as governor, made it his custom to walk from the Palace to attend services once a month with his staff, in full uniform. Perhaps he would say: "Go over to Christo Rey now and you can see the beautiful reredos that hung in the La Castrense." Yet, most stories are of a more recent time, and the sameness of the Wallace years can only be felt once again in the song of the mockingbirds, singing in the branches of the willows, grown great along the Bonito Valley; for here had passed the pageantry of the frontier—pioneers of the New World, Indians, soldiers of the old Army, descendants of Spanish conquerors. These trails were made by men with tiger hearts. Yet what remains are the vagrant winds that stir the grasses, or the dust-devils that come from nowhere, spin for a moment with a wild fury, and are themselves but an instant of the past.

The earliest known map of Santa Fe, drawn by Jose de Urrutia, around 1766-68 (Adams.)

The City Different and The Palace

The Palace of the Governors:
Its Role in Santa Fe History

Jesse Nusbaum (l.) and Charles Lummis, from a 1910 photograph taken in Central America.

Photograph taken at Frijoles Canyon in 1910 of some of the luminaries with the School of American Archaeology. Standing, l. to r., Prof. Robbins of Boulder, Colo.; Donald Beauregard Ogden, artist; J.P. Harrington, linguist; F.W. Hodge, director, Bureau of Ethnology; Edgar Lee Hewett; Neil Judd, camp manager; Maude Way, Denver; Barbara Freire-Marreco, Oxford student; seated, l. to r., S.G. Morley, archaeologist; Kenneth Chapman, artist; J. Adams, surveyor; Jesse Nusbaum; N. Goldsmith, a student; Judge Henderson of Boulder, a naturalist.

(Above) Kenneth Chapman at work in the Palace, 1913. (Below) Col. Ralph E. Twitchell, 1913.

(Above, left) Edgar Lee Hewett, 1913. (Above, right) artist Carl Lotave, whose murals graced the 1909-1913 restoration of the Palace. (Below) Judge John McFie. Note the mural by Carlos Vierra.

Julian and Maria Martinez making pottery in the patio of the Palace. Maria and Julian were among the Pueblo peoples who assisted in the construction of the Painted Desert exhibit (replicas of Taos and San Ildefonso pueblos) for the Santa Fe Railway Company for the 1915 World's Fair, San Diego.

(Above) Portal of the Palace, looking west. In this 1911 photo, the interior restoration is in progress, but the exterior has not been restored. (Below) The restored Palace, in a 1913 photo taken during a Sunday afternoon band concert, looking east.

(Above) This is the only known photograph, taken by Jesse in 1909, of the Palace showing the old Post Office sign. Photo was taken shortly before restoration work began. (Below) The Palace, looking east down Palace Ave., 1909.

A 1913 photo of the portal as clean-up was being conducted following the restoration. Jesse told me, "There was much interest, especially from the men, as the portal advanced to completion. When my motorcycle was out there [note Jesse's cycle in the street] they gathered around. More people used the Plaza when the portal was completed and the Plaza cleaned up."

Woodsellers in the Plaza, 1909. This was a regular custom at the time.

(Above) The Palace patio, looking east; 1913, just after the restoration. The top of the old Armory building shows on the left. Indians from the pueblos often stayed in the north rooms or camped in the patio. (Below) Conditions at the Palace in 1909 as Jesse Nusbaum began the restoration. The horse and animal debris in some places was above the sills.

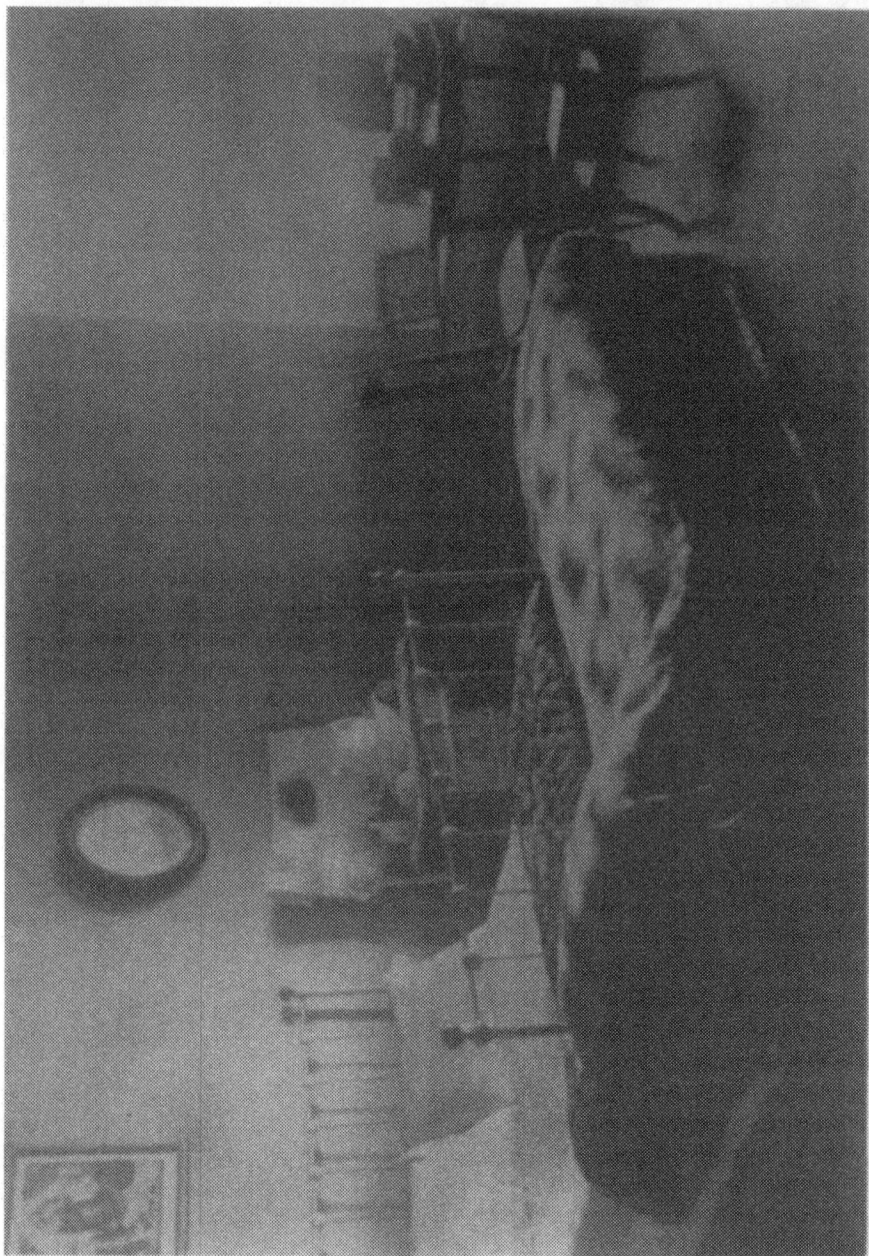

Governor Robert Ervien's bedroom in the Palace as Jesse first saw it in 1907.

Burros in the Palace patio. Old Elks' Club (now the Museum Administration building) visible at right. (1913).

The Pajarito Room in the Palace, 1913.

The Puje Room in the Palace with Carl Lotave's murals, 1913.

The Rito de los Frijoles Room, partially restored, 1913. Jesse had to narrow the ceiling gap in this room.

The Puye Room, 1913, with restoration completed. The Lotave murals are visible, and Jesse's display cases are completed.

The famous old post and corbel. Jesse noted, "This is the old post and corbel I found in the inner north wall in the Palace when it was necessary to rebuild this north wall of the former Ben Hur or Rito de los Frijoles Room in 1910. I later used this post and corbel as example for the restoration of the portal in the fall of 1913." (The Puye Room was done in late fall of 1909.)

The front room of the Palace after restoration; the window looks out on Washington Avenue. (This is the eastern-most room in what is called "the historical end" of the building.) (1913)

Two views of the 1910 DeVargas celebration in front of the Old Palace, prior to exterior restoration.

The Plaza on a summer afternoon in 1912. According to Jesse, this was taken "before the new bandstand was installed and right after the old one had been taken to Ft. Marcy."

The James Seligman home across from the Cathedral, 1909. Despite the exterior appearance of the Seligman house, the interior was very decorative. Next to the Seligman house was a two-story adobe, and next to that a red brick schoolhouse. The Exchange Hotel (not visible in the photo) at the corner of Shelby and San Francisco streets became the Rocky Mt. Camp Company, where horses could be rented.

The Big Dry Goods Store, seen here in 1908, was on San Francisco and Don Gaspar where Goodman's men's store now stands.

Looking east up Palace Avenue; Sena Plaza, before the portal was added, is on the left, and the familiar grounds of St. Vincent's Park is on the right (1909).

San Francisco Street, the Cathedral visible in the background, and what appears to have been a parade of some kind. (1908)

The old Exchange Hotel, historic meeting place for those who came over the trails to Santa Fe (1909). The La Fonda Hotel now stands on this spot.

The original Palace Hotel (1908), which has long since burned down.

Jesse's 1909 photograph of "The Oldest House" at the corner of Old Pecos Trail (formerly College Street) and DeVargas, across from the Chapel of San Miguel.

Burros laden with alfalfa, a common sight around 1908 when this photograph was taken. The First National Bank now stands at the site of the building in the background.

Ruins of the "Garita," on the hillside just east of the restored Morley house and below Fort Marcy (on Washington Avenue). This photograph was taken in 1909; nothing at all now remains of the ruins.

A full crop of pinon nuts is being hauled for shipping out by Gormley's General Store; 1913, Canyon Road.

Looking down on the city from the Federal building (the rounded fence in the foreground surrounds the Court House, then being completed). In this 1914 photo, the old bandstand from the Plaza is discernible on Ft. Marcy hill, just right of center.

Looking up at Ft. Marcy from Hillside Ave. This is a fine shot of the "Shitti Corral." According to Jesse's notes, the name lasted since the beginning of Santa Fe. A public petition was circulated in an attempt to rename the place "Escalone," but the move was defeated and the city fathers' pronouncement was "All the flavor of the past must remain." (1913)

This long-distance view of Santa Fe was taken by Jesse in 1912. The Clark House is in the right foreground, and the Federal Court House and Cathedral are visible in the distance.

A Pueblo woman completes restoration of a fireplace in the Palace; taken during restoration of the Palace, 1912.

The old Pigeon place near Apache Pass and how it looked in the early 1900s.

CHAPTER II

THE TERRITORIAL PALACE

WHY THE PALACE OF THE GOVERNORS IS NOT PART OF THE SMITHSONIAN INSTITUTION

by

Richard B. Woodbury

(The following article originally appeared in EL PALACIO, Summer 1969, and is reprinted with the permission of the Museum of New Mexico Press.)

When Clinton P. Anderson published his history of "The Adobe Palace" he ended the story in 1900, when Miguel A. Otero, Governor of the Territory of New Mexico, wrote to the Secretary of the Interior, Ethan A. Hitchcock, "I am still of the opinion that the old palace building ought to go back to the government who could properly care for it. I am very much afraid that if it is not turned back it will go to rack and ruin . . . I have always thought that this historical old building should have been made a branch of the Smithsonian Institution." Soon after this, Governor Otero nearly succeeded in accomplishing just this, failing for reasons that have remained hidden in the correspondence files of the Smithsonian and only recently encountered.

In 1900 the Palace had just passed from the federal government to the territory, owing to the enactment on June 21, 1898 of legislation transferring certain lands to the Territory of New Mexico, which specifically stated that "The building known as the Palace of the City of Santa Fe, and all lands and appurtenances connected therewith and set apart and used therewith, are hereby granted to the Territory of New Mexico."

Prior to this, as Senator Anderson has recounted, there had been many years of struggle among a distinguished series of antagonists over the use of the Palace. At various times parts of it were occupied by the Second National Bank, the U.S. Depository, the U.S. Post Office, the Texas, Santa Fe and Northern Railway, the Historical Society of New Mexico, and various individuals who made their residence there, besides its traditional official use by the Governors and Legislature of New Mexico.

The means by which Governor Otero attempted to achieve his own particular destiny for the Palace was House Joint Resolution No. 7, passed by the Territorial Legislature on March 20, 1901. This read as follows:

Whereas, the building in the City of Santa Fe, known as the Palace, is the oldest public building and the most historic edifice in the United States, having been the seat of governmental power and the home of the executive officials of New Mexico, through all the changes in government for three centuries; and

Whereas, New Mexico itself is more prolific in A[r]chaeological treasures than any other part of the Union, and has already contributed more largely than any other state or territory to the National Museum; and it is desirable that its peculiar historical objects should be preserved in one place, and amid their natural environment, instead of being scattered all over the world, and

Whereas, the Territorial Legislatures of 1882 and 1884, asked that this historic edifice be devoted to the preservation of the antiquities of New Mexico, and two Secretaries of the Interior have officially recommended that its permanent use be that of a museum of the antiquarian collections of the Southwest, and

Whereas, by inadvertence in the wording of the Act of Congress which donated public lands to the Territory for educational and other purposes passed June 21, 1898, the Palace property was included in the cession made by the United States to New Mexico without any wish for such cession on the part of our people, and

Whereas, the two Houses of the last Legislature, each by a unanimous vote, passed a joint resolution, asking the United States to reassume ownership of said property and that a western branch of the National Museum be established at the Palace.

Now, therefore, be it resolved (if the Council concur), that this Legislature considers that the appropriate future of the Palace should be as the home of the great collections, of Archaeological and other antiquities of New Mexico and the Southwest.

Resolved, That we request the authorities in charge of the National Museum of the Smithsonian Institution, to establish a Southwestern Museum of the character hereinbefore indicated as the Palace property with the ancient Palace itself as the center.

Resolved: That the Territorial Board of Public Lands be authorized and directed to convey said palace property either to the United States or to the Smithsonian Institution, upon condition that a branch either of the National Museum, or the Museum of the Smithsonian Institution be established and maintained therein; that the Palace building be preserved in good order, and without material changes in its general structure and appearance forever; that the New Mexico Historial Society be allowed such space in said building as it may require for the proper exhibition of its collection of New Mexico antiquities and other objects illustrating the history of the Territory, as a part of said general exhibition; that the exhibition rooms in said building be open to the public without charge forever and that no expense for arrangement or maintenance of said building and its contents be a charge on New Mexico or any civil division thereof.

Benjamin M. Read
Speaker of the House

J. Franco. Chaves
President of the Council

R.L. Baca
Chief Clerk of the House

W.E. Martin
Chief Clerk of the Council

Approved by me this 20th day of March A.D. 1901.

Miguel A. Otero
Governor of New Mexico.

Filed in Office of Secretary of New Mexico, Mar. 20, 1901 at 1:30 p.m.

Geo. H. Wallace
Secretary

A copy of this joint resolution, with an elegant certificate of its correctness . . . was sent to the Smithsonian Institution, where it was received on April 3, 1901 and referred to the Secretary. We can assume that Governor Otero had every expectation that the Smithsonian would promptly accept this offer. For one thing, Vice-President Theodore Roosevelt was an ex-officio member of the Smithsonian's Board of Regents, and, as Twitchell expressed it: ". . . the well known personal relations existing between the president and Governor Otero . . . were of the most friendly character." (P. 522) This friendship, and Roosevelt's respect for Otero, derived from the assistance that Otero had given in organizing the troops in New Mexico which became part of the Rough Riders under Colonel Roosevelt's command in the Spanish-American war. Also, as Twitchell points out, Otero received the "unsought endorsement of his administration of New Mexican affairs by ex-officers of that famous regiment, many of whom the governor saw fit to appoint to more or less lucrative or honorary offices within the patronage of the executive."

However, the favorable response that the Smithsonian's Regents might have made never came because of a combination of accidental and bureaucratic events beyond the control of any person. The first step in the Smithsonian's leisurely consideration of New Mexico's offer was, however, a favorable one. Secretary Samuel P. Langley immediately sent the proposal to John Wesley Powell, Director of the Bureau of American Ethnology, who replied on April 22 that ". . . the resolution constitutes a tender of valuable property, which is of much historic interest in addition to the monetary value, to the Smithsonian Institution under conditions of remarkable liberality." He continued with his opinion "that it would be feasible and in some respects advantageous (at least for some years to come) to maintain a collaborator of this Bureau at Santa Fe in charge of the building and the collections therein, should such a course seem expedient to the Secretary." After expressing the view "that acceptance would be wise and in accordance with 'the increase and diffusion of knowledge among men,'" he suggested that Frederick W. Hodge's views be asked, since he was well acquainted with the building "and with the conditions attending the proposed transfer."

Hodge's views were indeed asked, and they were transmitted to Secretary Langley in a five page report on May 4th, 1901. As would be expected, Hodge was enthusiastic about the prospect and provided numerous details—probably the first specific information on the nature of the Palace of the Governors that Langley had had. After briefly outlining the history of the building, he wrote:

The building occupies the entire northern frontage of the plaza, or public square, and may be regarded as among the most valuable property in Santa Fe, even if considered only from a pecuniary point of view. The walls are constructed of adobe, covered with cement plaster, I think and are very massive. The western end is occupied by the City Post Office, for use of which the Government pays $600.00 per year rental. Near the eastern end a room or two are rented by a lawyer. In the extreme eastern end are the rooms of the Historical Society of New Mexico, which pays no rental, but which maintains an excellent but badly classified and poorly labelled collection of historical and archaeological objects, mainly local in character.

In the rear of the Palace is a yard with some low buildings at the back in a poor state of preservation. Farther to the rear (i.e. northward) and extending the full width of the block, is an alfalfa field, perhaps a couple of hundred feet in width. That alfalfa crop I understand, has always been regarded as a perquisite of the Secretary of the Territory, but of its value, I know nothing. This ground forms a part of the Palace property.

The benefits to be derived by the Smithsonian Institution from obtaining this property would probably become greater as time went on. I am not informed what income from the Palace is now available through rental [here, a footnote in Hodge's hand has been added, stating "$912 per year. See attached letter."]. Probably it would not be more than sufficient to keep the building in proper repair; but it seems to me quite possible that the residence formerly occupied as the Fort Marcy officers' quarters, etc., situated north of the alfalfa field and now under control of the Department of the Interior, could be obtained without cost, thus affording an income at least sufficient for maintenance and probably large enough to enable archaeologic and other field work to be accomplished for the benefit of the National Museum.

Regarding the exhibit which the Legislature is desirous of having maintained, I think it is the intention of the people to have the collections of the Historical Society of New Mexico form a nucleus. The principal item of expense connected with the entire project will be the employment of a custodian; but if the proper person were selected, important collections could be made from time to time, both through gift and by excavation, at least half the objects being transferred to the National Museum. It is quite probable that the railroad companies could be induced to cooperate with the Institution in maintaining the exhibit proposed by transporting specimens from all sections in New Mexico to Santa Fe free of cost, or at greatly reduced rates. I believe it would be quite possible for me to make such an arrangement with the Atchison, Topeka and Santa Fe Railroad Company, which has always been very liberally inclined toward scientific students.

Even if the Institution finds it not possible to make the project self-supporting for a few years, I still think that great good would be done were it to accept this generous offer of the people of New Mexico, who have always guarded their historic Palace with reverential care. Its acceptance could scarcely fail to redound to the glory of the Institution as it would surely result in the enrichment of the collections of the National Museum.

Finally, Hodge suggested that the Smithsonian might send a representative to Santa Fe to obtain fuller information on the subject—which was not done, so far as can be determined. However, only the previous summer Hodge, "with a party of volunteer assistants comprising" Elliott Coues, George Parker Winship, and A.C.

Vroman, had made a lengthy trip to the existing pueblos and to the ruins of New Mexico and Arizona, collecting data and photographs for the "Cyclopedia of Native Tribes" (BAE 1903: pp.x-xi) which later was published as the well-known *Handbook of American Indians North of Mexico.*

Probably as useful as a trip to visit the Palace of the Governors was the letter attached to Hodge's report and referred to in his footnote, quoted above. This was a short, hand-written communication from L. Bradford Prince, addressed to "Prof. F.W. Hodge" and written on May 13, 1901, on the letterhead of The Bureau of Immigration of the Territory of New Mexico, Office of the Secretary. (The back of this stationery carried a full page of information in small type, headed "Resources of New Mexico," and including Fruit, Sugar Beets, Minerals, Mineral Springs, Desirable Lands, etc.). Although no letter from Hodge to Prince has been found in the Smithsonian files, Hodge had presumably requested the information specifically, as well as been in touch with Prince about the entire proposal. Prince wrote as follows:

> My dear Sir:
> By rough measurement the Palace property is as follows: Front on Plaza 255 feet—depth of main building, about 42 feet. Entire depth of grounds 270 feet; of which the Palace building & corral includes 110 feet. [Here Prince included a rough sketch showing the dimensions just given, and indicating that the Palace occupied the southern quarter of the tract and beyond the "corral wall" the alfalfa field occupied the northern half, with "Military Reservation" and "Present Governor's Residence" adjacent on the north.] The P.O. is rented to U.S. at $600 a year. 2 offices in center at $13 each per month—Total rental $912.
> As it is untaxed, this is more than ample for repairs, etc.
> Everything *now* is favorable for the transfer, and I think it should be pushed through; as it is never possible to say what obstacles may arise in the future from selfishness & cupidity.
>
> Your h s [?]
>
> L. Bradford Prince

As far as the official correspondence shows, Secretary Langley's reaction to Hodge's enthusiastic report and the details furnished by Prince was not encouraging. He wrote to Hodge on May 18, complimenting him on his report but saying that acceptance by the Smithsonian of a building "in a distant Territory" would be "a wide departure from its course of action in all its past history." He commented on the possible expenses that might be involved and concluded that "it should be undertaken, if at all, only after much deliberation. The matter may even be of sufficient importance to require to be submitted to the Regents." And he asked Hodge to draft an acknowledgement to the Territory of New Mexico "deferring any immediate action or acceptance of responsibility on the part of the Institution." This Hodge did, and on May 21 Secretary Langley wrote to Governor Otero acknowledging receipt of House Joint Resolution Number 7 and saying that "the matter is now under consideration and that in due season a definite response to this greatly appreciated tender by the Legislature of New Mexico will be given by the Smithsonian Institution" (Smithsonian 4, 5: 167).

However, it is probable that Governor Otero regarded the official formalities of acknowledgment and consideration less important than the political realities that had made it possible for him to secure the joint resolution in the first place, at a time when his friend Theodore Roosevelt was a member of the Smithsonian's Board of Regents. But the Regents met only once a year (on the fourth Wednesday of each year) and it was already late in May, when for generations the thoughts of Washington's office holders, bureaucrats, and legislators have all turned to possibilities for a more kindly summer climate. Therefore, whatever further consideration the Territory's offer may have received, no official progress was likely until cooler weather and the next meeting of the Regents permitted. Instead, Governor Otero received an apologetic letter dated August 3, 1901, from Acting Secretary Rathbun, stating that the Secretary was "now absent from Washington" but that "before his departure the Secretary gave the matter such consideration as the generous tender on the part of the people of New Mexico deserves and the importance of the project demands." However, he said, a decision must await presentation of the question to the Board of Regents at their next meeting in January, 1902.

Before that meeting occurred, however, the membership of the Board of Regents was unexpectedly changed. On September 14, 1901, Roosevelt succeeded to the Presidency, due to the assassination of McKinley, and thus his membership on the Board ceased. In his place there was appointed William P. Frye, President Pro Tempore of the Senate. Neither Frye nor most of the other members of the Board had any particular reason to know of or be interested in Santa Fe's Palace or New Mexico's antiquities. Besides Chief Justice Melville W. Fuller, Chancellor of the Smithsonian Institution and President of the Board of Regents, there were three U.S. Senators, Shelby M. Cullom (Illinois); Orville H. Platt (Connecticut), and Francis M. Cockrell (Missouri)—all three of them lawyers—three members of the House of Representatives, Robert R. Hitt (Illinois; who had been for seven years First Secretary at our Embassy in Paris), Robert Adams, Jr. (Pennsylvania; a member of the U.S. Geological Survey party that explored the Yellowstone from 1871 to 1875, and later U.S. Minister to Brazil), and Hugh A. Dinsmore (Arkansas; a lawyer and former Minister to Korea) (Biographical Directory of the American Congress).

There were also three "citizens of a state," James B. Angell (former president of the University of Vermont and then President of the University of Michigan; also a founder and former president of the American Historical Society), Alexander D. White (founder and first president of Cornell University and at various times minister or ambassador to Germany and Russia; also a founder of the Carnegie Institution of Washington), and Richard Olney (Attorney-General and then Secretary of State under Cleveland, now in private law practice). Finally, there were three "citizen members" from Washington City, George Gray (who, after fourteen years as a Senator from Connecticut was now a U.S. Circuit Court judge), Alexander Graham Bell (best known for his invention of the telephone, but also a strong supporter of Langley's experiments with heavier-than-air flight), and John B. Henderson (a former Senator from Missouri, now retired and practicing law in Washington) (Dictionary of American Biography). Of these distinguished men, several had travelled abroad but only Adams had had first-hand contact with scientific explorations in the American West and only Angell and White are known to have the scholarly and historical interests that the present question required.

There is no doubt that at the Smithsonian F.W. Hodge, at least, was aware of the lack of strong support for acceptance of the Palace and the unfortunate effect that Roosevelt's departure from the Board of Regents had. For on January 31, 1901, Hodge had resigned from the Bureau of American Ethnology in order to become Assistant in Charge of the Office of the Smithsonian Institution, a role that necessarily involved him daily in the Smithsonian's administrative deliberations and actions. Although there is no relevant correspondence other than that already mentioned above for the autumn and early winter of 1901, the supporters of Governor Otero's efforts must have been active.

Bradford Prince, especially, was undoubtedly in touch with Hodge following his letter of the previous May since he was deeply concerned with New Mexico history and archaeology. Appointed by President Hayes to the chief justiceship of New Mexico in 1879, Prince resigned in 1882 and devoted himself to a variety of civic, commercial, agricultural and financial activities. He was active in the efforts to achieve statehood. He became president of the New Mexico Historical Society in 1883 and retained the position until his death.

Following his term as governor (1889-1893), Prince was active in numerous international expositions as well as a variety of professional and business organizations. His *Spanish Mission Churches of New Mexico*, published in 1915, was the most popular of his historical writings. As his letter of May 13 to Hodge indicates, he regarded 1901 as the critical moment to secure the transfer of the Palace to the Smithsonian, an undertaking of a sort in which he had already long been effective.

The only specific indication of the efforts that Prince made in behalf of the Joint Resolution is in copies in the Smithsonian's correspondence files of two long identical letters sent on January 15, 1902, to Regents Frye and Adams. They read in part as follows:

Dear Sir:

I beg to address you as one of the Regents of the Smithsonian Institution, on a subject in which all of those interested in historical and archaeological matters feel a deep concern; I refer to the permanent use of the Governor's Palace of this city, by your Institution, for a southwestern branch museum.

The building is altogether the most historic in the United States; a short sketch referring to this subject is enclosed. [This was probably an extract from Governor Prince's report of 1890 entitled "The Palace, Santa Fe, New Mexico, erected in 1598" of which a copy was filed with the present letter.]

The southwest is so full of objects of interest (as the large collections in Washington testify) that it is very desirable that at least a part of its antiquarian treasures should be preserved in their natural environment . . . This section will certainly be the scene of great activity in exploration and excavation for many years to come. Santa Fe is naturally the central point from which work will be directed, and to which its results will be brought.

I understand that a full report will be made on this subject as the coming of the Regents, and this, no doubt will include a description of the Palace. I enclose a photograph to give a better idea. At present, parts of it are rented as a post office, offices, &c. It is in very excellent order, a large sum having been expended by the territory during the last Fall in repairs, repainting &c. so that it never looked better.

I write to urge in the interest of historical and archeological science, that you accept this offer by the territory. If not, there is always a danger that in some legislature the mercantile spirit may prevail, and this venerable structure be destroyed, simply because the ground on which it stands is the most valuable in the city for mercantile purposes.

Very respectfully,

/s/ L. Bradford Prince
President, New Mexico Historical Society

Whether Prince wrote to others among the Regents in his final week before their meeting is not known, but his efforts were insufficient in any case. With Roosevelt not present, and, as far as can be determined, with little or no background information supplied to the Regents before or during their meeting, Secretary Langley apparently presented the matter in the most cautious, negative manner possible. The Minutes of the Proceedings at the Annual Meeting of the Board of Regents held January 22, 1902, as recorded in the attest copy deposited in the Smithsonian Archives tell the story briefly but clearly:

"Santa Fe Palace"

The Government of New Mexico had offered to transfer an ancient Spanish palace in Santa Fe, to the Institution on condition that the Institution maintained at no charge to the State a museum of Archaeology of the Southwest; and the Secretary had promised to refer the matter to the Board.

Now, the Secretary wishes to say to the Board, that there are probably various other schemes for making local museums at the expense of the National Government which were not unlikely to seek the help of the Institution. It was in this point of view that the application of the Government of New Mexico, which he now presented, was of importance as setting a precedent; and if the Regents were unable to give the matter their full attention now, the Secretary would respectfully suggest that they give some committee, with the Secretary, the power to act in the matter of laying down what may be a general policy in such cases, and to give a reply to the Governor's letter.

A discussion ensued in which the general view was opposed to the acceptance of the Palace, and Senator Frye moved that the matter be referred to a committee.

Before this motion was put, Mr. Adams said that he thought it would be best to meet the issue fairly now; that it was not possible to accept the offer on account of the lack of means, and that if accepted, it would establish a precedent and cause other things of the same kind to be put upon the Institution, which even now had difficulty in conducting its work owing to the smallness of its means.

Senator Frye withdrew his motion, and Mr. Adams moved that it be the sense of the meeting that the Board of Regents deem it inadvisable to accept the proposition.

The motion was carried.

Nearly a year after its beginning, the correspondence between the Territory of New Mexico and the Smithsonian Institution comes to an end, on a coldly formal note. Secretary Langley wrote to Governor Otero on February 20, 1902, that the Board of Regents ". . . at its annual meeting held the twenty-second ultimo, resolved that it was impracticable to accept the proposal of the Territory." He closed by stating that, "The Secretary begs to tender in behalf of the Regents their thanks for the kind offer of the people of New Mexico, as set forth in the resolution of the Legislature, bearing the approval of the Executive, and their regret in being compelled to regard unfavorably the proposed transfer of the Palace building." (Smithsonian 1-41:303). On February 25 Governor Otero acknowledged this communication formally and briefly. Secretary Langley, by adding the spectre of a precedent which would lead to a long series of "schemes" for saddling the Smithsonian with local museums, successfully led the Regents to the conclusion that he appears to have favored from the start. Bureaucratic caution had prevailed, although there is no doubt that the Institution's slender means were already strained by the demands placed on them. It was perhaps Frye's hope that more favorable action could be secured in the committee he suggested, but the degree of the Regents' lack of information or interest, as reflected in the quaint designation "an ancient Spanish palace in Santa Fe," prevailed over whatever support he or others might have mustered.

There is no doubt that the history of the Smithsonian and of the Palace might both have been altered by a favorable response to the resolution of the New Mexico legislature—a branch museum of archaeology, federal custody of the Palace, Smithsonian research programs centered in Santa Fe rather than initiated intermittently and from distant Washington. However, the Palace was not lost to "the mercantile spirit," as Prince had feared. Efforts in the next few years to have the Palace made a national monument, under the Antiquities Act of 1906, and to secure it as the permanent home of a School of American Archaeology, under the Archaeological Institute of America, were not successful.

Nevertheless, the Palace of the Governors has survived and has prospered as the nucleus of the Museum of New Mexico, and in a broader sense the aims of Governor Otero, L. Bradford Prince, and F.W. Hodge have been achieved.

THE SANTA FE ARCHAEOLOGICAL SOCIETY

From *El Palacio*, July 1946, Vol. LIII, No. 7. Reprinted by permission of the Museum of New Mexico Press.

Oldest archaeological society now in existence in the Southwest, the Santa Fe Archaeological Society began thinking of itself as more than a local organization in 1906; legally became the Archaeological Society of New Mexico in 1909; and was incorporated under this name in 1938.

Our introductory article ended with the newspaper report of the founding of this society on September 14, 1900 (see *El Palacio*, April, 1946, pp. 79-88). At a meeting of the society on February 1, 1901, Prof. Hewett gave a public lecture about the Pajarito plateau, and L. Bradford Prince offered a memorial to Congress asking that the Palace of the Governors be made a national museum "for the antiquities that will be found in Pajarito Park," which was unanimously approved. Mr. Prince, a year earlier, had introduced before the Historical Society resolutions "protesting against alterations in historic monuments and favoring the establishment by the United States government of a western national museum with headquarters in the Palace."

With the backing of both societies, Mr. Prince went to the New Mexico legislature. The result was Joint Resolution No. 7 of 1901, which asked the federal government to take over the Palace of the Governors, saying that the territorial legislatures of 1882 and 1884 had requested this historic edifice to be devoted to the preservation of the antiquities of New Mexico; that two secretaries of the Interior had officially recommended its permanent use as a museum of the antiquities of the Southwest; and that "by inadvertence in the wording of the act of Congress which donated public lands to the Territory for educational and other purposes passed June 21, 1898, the Palace property was included in the cession

75

made by the United States to New Mexico without any wish for such cession on the part of our people . . ." It asked that, since the two houses of the preceding legislature had passed a joint resolution inviting the United States to reassume ownership of the Palace, the property be considered as the home of the great collections of archaeology and other antiquities of New Mexico and the Southwest.

When the matter was still pending six years later, the *Santa Fe New Mexican* said, in retrospect: "The purport of the resolution, drafted by ex-Governor L.B. Prince, was to get rid of the Old Palace on the part of the Territory and to have established therein a branch of the . . . Smithsonian Institute. Nothing came of the matter, because there was no law under which the federal government could take over the Old Palace without special legislation by Congress."

Governor Miguel Otero, who was one of the first territorial officials to take an interest in archaeology, had been concerned for some time by the cost of upkeep on the venerable building. The general feeling was that if the federal government would take over this "white elephant" the state would be relieved of a large financial burden. With the public eye just beginning to open to local history and prehistory, credit is due to the handful of citizens who were doing the awakening, and to the idea of making the Palace of the Governors into a museum—which, as we shall see, had far reaching consequences.

On March 16, 1901, the newspaper said: "The last meeting of the season, and in some respects the most interesting meeting of the archaeological society, was held last evening in the supreme court room at the capitol. Judge McFie . . . was in the chair. Prof. E.L. Hewett lectured, reviewing the ground covered by the society at its previous meetings . . . and introduced much new and interesting material relative to the cliff dwellings . . . ."

Extract from the Bulletin of the Archaeological Institute of America:

SECOND ANNUAL REPORT OF
THE SCHOOL OF AMERICAN ARCHAEOLOGY, 1908-1909.

To the Council of the Archaeological Institute of America:

GENTLEMEN

Since the last meeting of the Council the School of American Archaeology has been permanently located at Santa Fe, New Mexico; it seems fitting therefore to present a brief account of the inception and development of the School up to the present time.

In 1905 attention was directed toward the American field through efforts to secure legislation to protect from spoliation the ruins of the Southwest. In these efforts the Archaeological Institute of America took an active part. Such a law had been urged upon the Congress for more than ten years, but previously no concerted action by institutions had been brought about. The result of these efforts was the "Lacey Bill," an Act for the Preservation of American Antiquities, (published in the American Journal of Archaeology. Vol. X, 1906, pp. 175, 176).

An increasing interest in American Archaeology among affiliated Societies of the Institute led President Seymour, at the Ithaca meeting in 1905, to cooperate actively with the Committee on American Archaeology in organizing the work in the American field. At the meeting of the Institute held in Washington in 1906, it was proposed that all the work in the American field be placed under an official, to be known as the Director of American Archaeology, and that a School should be founded as soon as possible. The plan was adopted by the Committee and ratified by the Council of the Institute, and Edgar L. Hewett was elected Director published in the Supplement of Volume XI, *American Journal of Archaeology* (1907), p. 51.

The next step was taken at the Chicago meeting of the Institute, when, on December 30, 1907, the Council passed a resolution establishing "The School of American Archaeology." By the same act the Committee on American Archaeology was made the Managing Committee of the School (Supplement to Volume XII, 1908, p. 44). The field operations during the season of 1908 were reported by the Director (Supplement to Volume XII, 1908, p. 48).

At a meeting of the Managing Committee held at Cambridge, Mass., November 14, 1908, it was voted to accept the tentative proposition from the Archaeological Society of New Mexico to locate the School in Santa Fe, provided that certain stipulations should be compiled with.

At the meeting of the Council of the Institute in Toronto, December 31, 1908, the following revision of the Act of 1907, by which the School of American Archaeology was established was adopted:

1. "The School of American Archaeology is established to conduct the researches of the Institute in the American field, and to afford opportunities for field work and training to students of archaeology.

2. "The School will direct the expeditions of the local Societies in their respective fields, maintain archaeological researches in the various culture areas of the American continent, direct the work of fellows, and collaborate with universities and other scientific organizations, both home and foreign, in the advancement of archaeological research.

3. "The Committee heretofore known as the Committee on American Archaeology, with additional members as hereinafter provided for, shall become the Managing Committee of the School. The Committee shall consist of twenty-eight members, elective, and the following ex officio members: The President, Secretary, and Treasurer of the Institute, the Chairman of the Managing Committees of the American Schools in Athens, Rome, and Palestine, and the Chairman of the Committees on Medieval and Renaissance Studies. The Committee shall have power, with the ratification of the Council, to elect its own members and to fill all vacancies in its membership. The term of office shall be for four years, and the terms of not more than seven members shall expire in any one year. There shall be an Executive Committee consisting of the Chairman, Secretary, and Treasurer of the Managing Committee, the President of the Institute, and five elective members. The Committee shall appoint the Director of American Archaeology, who shall be its Executive Officer and Director of the School. The Committee is authorized to maintain Fellowships, archaeological stations, publications and the various lines of work herein provided for, and to raise funds for the support of same. Its funds shall be held by the Treasurer of the Institute, and disbursed by him on the order of the Chairman of the Managing Committee, approved by the President of the Institute."

On February 19, 1909, the Legislature of New Mexico passed the following Act, which practically complied with the stipulations contained in the communications sent by the Managing Committee of the Archaeological Society of New Mexico.

AMENDED HOUSE BILL NO. 100

An Act, Entitled "An Act to Establish a Museum for the Territory of New Mexico, and for other purposes."

WHEREAS, The Archaeological Institute of America, located in the City of Washington, D.C., a corporation organized and existing under and by virtue of an act of the Congress of the United States, has be a resolution adopted by the Council of the said Institute on the 31st day of December, 1908, made a proposition to the Territory of New Mexico, for the location of its School of American Archaeology in Santa Fe, which proposition is filed with the Secretary of New Mexico, and upon the performance of the conditions thereof by the Archaeological Institute of America all of the provisions of this Act are based: and

WHEREAS, the said Territory of New Mexico is desirous of accepting the proposition made by said Institute and availing itself of the benefits of said Territory arising therefrom: Therefore—Be it enacted by the Legislative Assembly of the Territory of New Mexico:

Section 1. There is hereby established the Museum of New Mexico, which shall be located in the City of Santa Fe, and which shall be under the management and control of a board of regents of six members to be appointed as hereinafter provided.

Section 2. The building known as the Old Palace in Santa Fe, and the grounds appertaining thereto, bounded as follows: On the South by Palace Ave.: On the East by Washington Ave.: On the North by lands of the Territory on which is now being constructed the Armory Building and the lands of the Santa Fe Lodge No. 460, B.P.O.E. of Santa Fe, and on the West by Lincoln Ave., together with all buildings and improvements thereupon situate and all lands or other property that may be acquired for Museum purposes at any time in the future, are hereby placed under the control of the Board of Regents herein created, for the use of the Museum herein established, and for other purposes as herein specified.

Section 3. The Board of Regents shall grant, free of rent, to the Archaeological Institute of America, the use of the property herein described, for the seat of its School and Museum of American Archaeology, which Museum shall be the Museum of New Mexico: Provided, That the rooms in the East end of the building which are now occupied by the Historical Society of New Mexico, shall be reserved for the use of said society, free of rent, so long as the same is conducted in harmony with the management of the Museum of New Mexico herein established, and for free public use; "The facts of which shall be judged of by the Territorial Legislature."

Section 4. The Board of Regents shall be constituted as follows: The Governor of New Mexico is hereby authorized to nominate, and by and with the advice and the consent of the council, appoint one reputable citizen of New Mexico, and three members of the managing committee of the School of American Archaeology, who shall be designated to him by its chairman. The Governor of New Mexico and the President of the New Mexico Archaeological Society shall be ex officio members of said Board of Regents, with full powers of membership. No member of said Board of Regents shall receive any salary or compensation, either directly or indirectly, from the Territory of New Mexico, for any services performed as members of said Board of Regents, and each member of said board shall after his appointment as aforesaid, take and subscribe an oath before a qualified notary public having a seal, for the faithful performance of his duties as such, which oath of office shall be filed with the Secretary of New Mexico. Said Board of Regents shall assemble at Santa Fe, New Mexico, within ninety days after the passage of this act, and organize by the election of one of its members as President, and one of its members as Secretary and Treasurer. The Secretary and Treasurer shall be a resident of New Mexico, and shall execute good and sufficient bond in the sum of not less than five thousand dollars to the Territory of New Mexico, to be approved by the Secretary of New Mexico, and by him deposited for safe keeping, for the faithful performance of his duties as Secretary and Treasurer as aforesaid, and for the proper accounting for all funds received by him from any source whatsoever in his official capacity. At the annual meeting of said Board of Regents, the accounts of the Secretary and Treasurer shall be audited, and all valid accounts approved. Four members of the Board of Regents shall constitute a quorum for the transaction of business, but a less number may adjourn from time to time. Said board shall provide proper rules and regulations for its own government. The appointed numbers of said board shall hold office for the term of four years, and until their successors are appointed and qualified. In case of any vacancy in said board, the Governor is hereby authorized to fill such vacancy in the same manner as provided for in this act, as to resident or non-resident appointive members.

Section 5. The Board of Regents shall accept the services of the Director of the School of American Archaeology as Director of the Museum of New Mexico, but said Director shall receive no salary from funds appropriated by New Mexico.

Section 6. The Board of Regents is authorized to equip the Old Palace building with heating plant, electric light and plumbing, out of funds to be appropriated for that purpose by the Territory of New Mexico, in a sum not to exceed three thousand dollars.

Section 7. The Board of Regents is directed that all alterations, extensions and additions to the main Palace building shall be made so as to keep it in external appearance as nearly as possible in harmony with the Spanish architecture of the period of its construction, and preserve it as a monument to the Spanish founders of the civilization of the Southwest.

Section 8. There is hereby provided an annual appropriation of five thousand dollars, or so much thereof as may be required to be used for the care and improvement of the building, grounds and museum, the obtaining of collections, books and equipment for the museum, the excavation and study of ancient ruins for the benefit of the museum, the preservation of archaeological sites in New Mexico, the publication of investigations in New Mexico, and for incidental expenses to the administration of the museum: Said appropriation to be available each year as follows: Twenty-five hundred dollars on the 30th day of June, and twenty-five hundred dollars on the 31st day of December, and the auditor of public accounts of New Mexico is hereby directed to make a sufficient levy on all property subject to taxation in New Mexico each year, to realize the sum provided herein, and to direct the several collectors of taxes to collect the same at the same time and in the same manner as other taxes are collected, and when the same shall be paid over to the territorial treasurer, he shall deposit the same in separate account to be kept by him to be known as "The Museum of New Mexico Fund," and the said auditor of public accounts shall draw his warrants on such funds when available on vouchers properly signed by the secretary and treasurer of said Board of Regents and the treasurer shall pay the same on presentation thereof to him.

Section 9. The Board of Regents of the Museum of New Mexico provided for by this Act shall make annually on or before the fifteenth day of January to the Governor of New Mexico a detailed report of all of its acts, transactions, receipts and disbursements for the calendar year immediately preceding such report, which said report shall be transmitted to the first session of the Legislative Assembly held after he shall have received the same for the consideration and action of the Legislature thereon. "The Museum of New Mexico hereby established and all of its property of every kind and description shall be and remain the exclusive property of the Territory of New Mexico, and any future legislature shall have the right to amend, alter or repeal this act in whole or in part."

Section 10. This act shall be in force and effect from and after its passage and all acts and parts of acts in conflict with any of the provisions of this act are hereby repealed and nothing in this act shall be construed in any way to interfere with the museums of the territorial institutions.

(Signed)   E.A. Miera,
             Speaker of the House of Representatives.
             E.H. Salazar,
             Chief Clerk of the House of Representatives.
             Chas. A. Spiess,
             President of the Council.
             Wm. F. Brogan,
             Chief Clerk of the Council.

Approved February 19th, 1909.
Nathan Jaffa,
Acting Governor for the Territory of New Mex.

Filed in the Office of Secretary of New Mexico, Feb. 19, 1909, 4 P.M.
Nathan Jaffa, Secretary.

At a meeting held in February, the Executive Committee nominated for appointment by the Governor of New Mexico, Dr. R.W. Corwin, Hon. Frank Springer, and Dr. Chas. F. Lummis, to act as Regents of the Museum of New Mexico. These nominations were confirmed and the Board of Regents met for organization in April. The Regents of the Museum held their first annual meeting in August at Puye Ruins, where excavations by the School were in progress. The Chairman spent a part of August and September in Santa Fe, and also visited the excavations.

The staff of the Museum and School is at present composed as follows:

Dr. Edgar L. Hewett, Director; Adolph F. Bandelier, Documentary History; Byron Cummings, Excavations in Utah and Arizona; Kenneth M. Chapman, Secretary and Illustrating Department; Sylvanus G. Morley, Archaeology of Central America; John P. Harrington, Ethnology; Jesse L. Nusbaum, Architectural Reconstruction and Photography; Carl Lotave, Artist.

The field work of the School during the present session and the various archaeological activities of the Affiliated Societies are given in the report of the Director of American Archaeology and of the School, herewith presented.

Respectfully submitted,
Alice C. Fletcher, Chairman.

Recommended by the Governor had been, Lummis, Corwin, Jaffa, and Springer.

CHAPTER III

THE RESTORATION OF THE PALACE
Including Jesse Nusbaum's Journals as Edited by the Author

On September 5, 1884, the Honorable A.R. Green, special agent of the Interior Department, sat in the Palace and penned this letter to the Honorable F.G. Adams, Secretary of the Kansas Historical Society, quoting from the New Mexican Review of Sept. 19, 1884:

Dear Sir:
    I have fragments of some of the skeletons of the seventy pueblo warriors who were shot in front of the Governor's Palace in Santa Fe, by order of Don Diego de Vargas, captain general of New Spain, on the 27th of December, 1692, which I propose to give your society if you care to have them. These Indians were buried in the placita, or court of the Palace, and it is believed their bones rested in peace until the last few years, when it became necessary to lay gas and water pipes for the use of the Palace. In digging, the workmen came upon the remains of the dead, and a number of skulls and bones were exhumed. The Palace was besieged with the curious and relic hunters, and Governor Seldon very properly forbade further search. Upon my request, however, in the name of our society, he cheerfully granted me the privilege, and those bones were discovered and dug up by a party of us in the 3d instant. There cannot be a shadow of doubt as to their genuiness."

Matters were moving rapidly when the glowing letter appeared in the *Daily New Mexican* of December 6, 1890, p. 5, from the Museum News Letter (and left from this time as it was found by Jesse Nusbaum almost exactly as here reported except for the change of occupants; eighteen years had elapsed when the Nusbaum restoration of 1909-13 began and the debris had only grown higher, to the window ledges in the patio). "The improvements on the historic adobe palace which have been in progress for the past five weeks have been finished and the building turned over to the secretary of the territory, who had only $3000 at his disposal for this work. The entire structure has been rebuilt as to foundation, unsightly cornices hard plastered and calsomined. Every inch of woodwork received 3 coats of paint, while the roofing is all brand new. The rooms are finished in hard plaster, rough coat, and calsomined with most exquisite tints, and many of the dwelling apartments to be used by the governor have been rather handsomely finished with rich paper ceilings, broad friezes and painted to match. For instance, in the reception room a soft tint of yellow predominates, in the dining room everything tends to pea green, in the main hall the colors are more sober, while the family bedroom is a bright blue and the library dark maroon. The whole building has thus been overhauled and modernized. Governor Prince and family will move into the unoccupied portion of the building in a few weeks."

It should be mentioned that the muslin they had stretched to cover the vigas, and plastered over with wallpaper to resemble eastern homes, it was said, were found by Nusbaum to be deplorable. The tendency was a sagging that left one to wonder that it held, and the new roofing had been the Tailor-tin edge standing type, leaving the many mice a roomy scampering place and home.

But Governor Otero was not pleased by the whole situation. Once again, October 31st, 1900, he wrote the secretary of the interior and stated: "I am still of the opinion that the old palace building ought to go back to the government who could properly care for it. I am very much afraid that if it is not turned back it will go to rack and ruin. I have always thought that this historical old building should have been made a branch of the Smithsonian Institution."

But the determination of the governor did not prevail. The Historical Society had fought too long and hard for a home. It desired to have display rooms for both scientific and historical materials they had and were accumulating.

In 1907-08, while serving as a professor of science and the manual arts at Las Vegas Normal University, Jesse Nusbaum, travelling by motorcycle, visited the Pajaritan Plateau. He spent ten days on foot and camping, with Santiago Naranjo of Santa Clara Pueblo as guide, on a photographic reconnaissance of the major ruins between Puye and Rito de los Frijoles.

In July 1909, Nusbaum and S.G. Morley, with the assistance of Indians from the nearby pueblos and under the direction of Edgar Lee Hewett, began the survey and excavation at the base of Puye Cliff, completely covered by the talus slopes. This was the first work on a large scale that had been done on New Mexico ruins of this size, and the scientific world began to notice a new and important class of architectural remains in the Southwest.

These "talus pueblos" constitute a large portion of the prehistoric sites in the Rio Grande valley. Soon the first members of the School of American Archaeology were headquartered for the summer period at Rito de los Frijoles. The Museum of New Mexico in the Palace of the Governors at Santa Fe, now housing newly restored workshops and an artist's studio, served as the base from which investigations and studies could take place at the Pajaritan Plateau. This need for a working base had played a great part in the Legislature's acquisition of the Palace for Museum purposes.

The season of 1909 was a busy one for the School, with Nusbaum directing restoration and clean-up at the Palace and work at Pajarito.

Now let us hear the story of the restoration in Jesse Nusbaum's own words:

I have always found the structure of the Palace the most interesting in the Southwest. Its current massive walls evolved over a period of four cultures and withstood the ravages of time very well. Originally, the Palace was the most imposing and important part of the royal presidio; an all-purpose fortress built by the followers of Don Pedro de Peralta. It extended east and west along the north side of the plaza for a distance of 400 feet, and north and south more than double that distance. The entire area had been surrounded by an adobe wall, and all of the buildings within this enclosure were known in early Spanish times as the Casas Reales. These had included the Palace proper, soldier's quarters, and several government structures.

A pair of low towers stood at either end on the Plaza side of the Palace. The west tower was used for the storage of powder and military equipment and the east tower housed a chapel for the use of the garrison. Adjoining and connecting the tower to its west end were the dungeons.

When the Americans came they enclosed it in a white picket fence; reduced it to its present size, planted alfalfa, and built two-story adobe buildings with portals supported by spindly columns on the three sides confronting the Palace. In 1909 I found the Plaza surrounded by an odd assortment of buildings, some ugly remnants of the early days housing various businesses.

The old Army Officer's barracks stood on the corner of Lincoln and Palace Avenue of adobe and frame construction in Territorial style, in poor condition, with its Territorial coping of brick in disrepair. It stood some six feet back from the sidewalks with portales on the east and south sides. The west end had second stories, and in 1909 it was only partly occupied with a few offices and rooms in rental. (On April 17, 1916 serving as archaeologist and superintendent of construction, I began dismantling this old Army Officer's barracks with a force of 36 men and 20 teams of wagons, and commenced the construction of the replica of the early Franciscan Missions on this site, for use as an Art Museum and Auditorium for the City of Santa Fe. Following archaeological scrutiny the materials were taken to the new three-storied building, which was to have housed the first unit of the University, then proposed for Santa Fe and still standing and which became the convent in the vicinity of the old D & RG, little brick railway station, one block south on Montezuma Avenue. To the rear of the old Army Officer's barracks at this time, a row of official Army Officers' residences of Fort Marcy stood, of adobe and frame construction, extending the length of the city block, north to Marcy Street.)

During the summer of 1907-08, I had been archaeologist and photographer under Dr. Edgar L. Hewett, then field director for the Archaeological Institute of America's exploratory expedition to the Mesa Verde National Park and in the McElmo Canyon and Hovenweep areas to the west thereof in 1908. At this time Hewett told me that the New Mexico Legislature had just approved a bill authorizing the establishment of the Museum of New Mexico and would house the Archaeological Institute of America's Archaeology therein, under his jurisdiction as Director ... that he wanted me as his first staff member as archaeologist-superintendent of construction and photographer.

The Act to establish a Museum for the Territory of New Mexico was approved on February 19, 1909 and placed under the management and control of a Board of Regents the old building known as the Old Palace in Santa Fe, and authorized said Board of Regents to equip the Old Palace with a heating plant, add further electric lights and plumbing, in a sum not to exceed $3,000 and also to provide an annual appropriation of $5,000 available June 30, and December each year, for the care and improvement of the building, grounds, and Museum and all other detailed purposes and objectives.

Early in June of 1909, I expressed my personal effects and photographic equipment from Las Vegas, New Mexico, where I had been Professor of Science and the Manual Arts through the College periods in 1907-08. I rode my four-horsepower, twin-cylinder, chain-belt-driven, two-speed Excelsior motorcycle over the rough and rocky Santa Fe Trail route, to enter on duty July 1 at the old Palace of the Governors. I was the first resident member of Director Hewett's staff. Within a few days Sylvanus G. Morley of Harvard arrived, to be the first member of the School of American Archaeology staff.

For some years the Palace of the Governors had been deteriorating very rapidly. I had approved the effort to stem the tide of nondescript architecture for Santa

Fe. The palace was begun with an adaptation to climate and atmosphere and had been fitted into the color of earth and sky. Here was a need to eliminate excrescences, substituting nothing and holding to the old natural lines.

This venerable building of great historical importance should beyond doubt be preserved in all integrity and perpetuated for all time. It was believed because of interest aroused that it should make excellent housing for both the School of American Archaeology staff and for a Museum of New Mexico. The Legislature, when conveying the building to the Museum of New Mexico, had provided very meagre funds for its operation. As a result the Archaeological Institute offered to pay the salary of the Director, who would also serve the Museum of New Mexico at no cost.

In 1609, Don Pedro de Peralta had laid out the Plaza and built the Palace of the Governors. This structure is the main and only surviving part of the once extensive Casa Reales (Royal Houses) constructed about 1610 as a fortress and seat of government of the Spanish Province of New Mexico. For 300 years it was the residence and official headquarters of the Governors of New Mexico under four successive flags—the Kingdom of Spain (1610-1821), the Empire of New Mexico (1821-1822), the Republic of Mexico (1823-1846), and the United States Territory of New Mexico (1846-1907). On February 19, 1909 by Act of the Legislature it became the first unit of the Museum of New Mexico. It is the oldest public building still in use in the nation.

In 1680 it had been seized by the Pueblo Indians, who burned every other building in Santa Fe, then made a multi-storied pueblo of the Casas Reales. They held it for thirteen years, after driving the Spanish out of New Mexico. The puddled-walls I uncovered would indicate pre-Spanish construction. Upon the reconquest of New Mexico in 1692-93 by Don Diego de Vargas, he restored and fortified the Casas Reales.

I found a document dated 1703 which refers to this section of the Casas Reales as El Palacio Real—the Royal Palace. It was so called until the American conquest of 1846, after which it was renamed the "Adobe Palace." Somewhat later we find it called "The Palace of the Governors."

Records show that it was occupied by the United States Army in 1846; this structure was 50 feet longer, east to west, than it is now. They then had a "calobozo," or jail, at the western end, where we know that in 1807 Major Zebulon M. Pike, U.S. Army, was held, el que ha estado.

Beyond the "Placita" in the rear extended the service buildings, stables, gardens, an old Spanish army barracks and officers' quarters serving Fort Marcy, which was the military headquarters-post for the Territory. For a brief period of two months in 1862, the Palace was occupied by the Confederate forces of Sibley. In the 1860's and 1870's the Palace was greatly rebuilt and "improved," but as if at random. Wall copings and Victorian woodwork, including the elaborate balustraded portal, were added. It was the intent of all involved in the rebuilding that some of the Territorial features be preserved where feasible.

In my first morning session with Dr. Hewett, at his residence, he summarized for me generally the current status of the planning of two new significant archaeological exhibit rooms, including tentative room locations for library, public assembly and lectures, and administrative office for the Director and Regents, plus a business and information office and a single studio with skylight for scientific research or

84

use by an artist. He regretted the mandatory reservations for sole use of the Historical Society of three large and two medium-size rooms, plus an entry corridor. In this context, he instructed me promptly to prepare a measured and scaled floor plan of the Old Palace proper, showing the locations of all existing doors, windows and fireplaces, etc., and to plot thereon proposed locations of interior steam pipeline loops and connecting radiators.

The afternoon session was held at the Old Palace. First I accompanied Dr. Hewett through the jumbled mass of the Historical Society exhibits in the east portion and there met the caretaker-custodian, Mr. Woodruff.

Enroute under the portal to the west end of the Palace, Dr. Hewett stated that the Historical Society would continue to exhibit its collections in the block of five rooms and the entrance-corridor in the eastern portion of the Palace. The major portion west thereof, which would house the School and its activities, including development of the Museum of New Mexico, was then totally occupied, except for one small room, by State officials and Federal Post Office.

The block of five rooms west of the Historical Society's quarters was occupied by Robert P. Ervien, Commissioner of Lands, his wife, and two young sons John and Howell. On the opposite side of the entrance corridor was the parlor, bedroom, and large closet of Territorial Governor George Curry and a small unused room opening off the joint Ervien and Curry entrance corridor. The largest room in the Palace and two connecting rooms were occupied by the Post Office, which had a contract with the Federal Government with another two years to go. It would be some months before it could be moved to a new location. Governor Curry would vacate his quarters as soon as the new Governor's Mansion was fully completed, and Commissioner Ervien hoped to move other quarters in advance thereof.

When later I met Governor Curry and the Erviens and arranged to make measured plans of the quarters they occupied, I ascertained they would welcome my use of the small room abutting the three rooms of Governor Curry as my temporary office and workroom. I set up my photographic equipment there and for some time slept on the floor in my sleeping bag, as my salary was a meagre $100 per month and I had decided to step up the sale of my photographs made into post cards, so that I might continue to record the many historic structures and the many interesting occasions in this area. [The Santa Fe New Mexican, Nov. 16, 1972. "Down the Old Santa Fe Trail" 60 years ago—on November 16, 1912: Jesse Nusbaum has just put out a beautiful line of Post Cards in colors, picturing scenes in and about Santa Fe. They are the prettiest I have ever seen of local views and are in the best Nusbaum vein, which is "Nuff Said."]

Because of my experience in construction, I immediately realized the great amount of work which had to be done to protect and preserve this structure. It was indeed in a sorry state. The walls were falling in many places, and everywhere inappropriate restorations were in evidence, a hodge-podge of ill-conceived additions conforming to no particular style of architecture. The plaza space behind the building had been filled up with trash and manure from the stabling of livestock in there, to such a level that it was well above the sills of the rear windows by a good deal and deeply eroded the walls at their base. I arranged for native workmen with teams for the immediate removal of this and it took 2100 small wagon loads for the removal of 1000 cubic yards of this material, to bring it down to a satisfactory level for grading and to insure proper drainage and stabilization of the base of the badly water-soaked and deteriorated walls, especially the north wall, with concrete and cobble-stone buttressing. All debris was carefully screened for archaeo-logical values "in situ" and then hauled to wherever fill was requested, the greater part going to the site of the proposed new University building on Montezuma Street.

The roof was in bad shape. Everything was in deplorable condition. There had been practically no expenditures for a long period of time on this building and I found myself working long into the night, developing the films I was taking at this time with my original top rank, 5"x7" double extension view-camera, equipped with Zeiss wide-angle and regular double element lenses and related accessories.

I continued the old habit of opening up my bed roll to sleep in my office, working very late at night. I can still smile at the memory of one early morning. About six-thirty a.m. somebody rang the Ervien's doorbell and I got up to answer it to find the older of the two Ervien boys, John, already there. I heard a woman tell him that she was from Boston and she introduced a young boy she held by the hand, as her son, Archibold. The boy asked to see the Ben Hur Room. John, to my great surprise, said, "Lady, that will be fifty cents for each of you." There had never been a charge for this since the time Governor Lew Wallace had written part of his famous book in this room, which had created much interest. I knew that Governor Curry was using this room as his bedroom and was not yet up. John, without any hesitation, led them through Governor Curry's office, into the door of his bedroom and literally to the foot of his bed, then stopped and said flatly, "This is the Ben Hur Room." The woman told her son Archibold to make a careful review of the room and all the things in it so he could tell his friends in Boston all about it. There was a small window in the room, but not enough light to see if anyone was in bed. The boy was looking about when suddenly Governor Curry roused up and sat up in bed. He had on an old-fashioned night shirt with red meander at the neck. The startled woman asked, "Who is that?" and John flatly answered, "Ben Hur himself." With that the woman turned on her heel, grabbed the boy by the hand, and out they went. John made a dollar on that. Governor Curry never phased at all, he simply went back down to finish out his sleep, but he told me later that he enjoyed this "house play" in which he participated.

As the result of a preliminary examination of the long unused and gravely deteriorated row of adobe rooms with dirt floors, deep and nearly filled pit-toilets, firewood and other open and closed storage rooms, across the north part of the patio, behind the Palace, built by the Army in 1867-1868 to replace former shelters, Dr. Hewett asked me to prepare a comprehensive scaled plan thereof. The sum of $3,000 was then available for this work. On the basis of this plan and related struc-tural findings, I was to submit an estimate of cost and repairing, reconstructing and converting each of these rooms and sheds into desperately needed workshops, laboratories and studios, as are not required for storage purposes and subterranean installation of the steam-furnace and large coal bin.

After ascertaining that the depth of the latrine accumulation was as much as eight feet and that removal would endanger the adobe walls, a heavy layer of lime and chloride of lime was applied over the latrine deposit, then covered to grade level with sand and said rooms were floored with evenly troweled cement. This was completed in 1909. From September through December, I supervised the installa-tion of the heating plant in the main Palace and began on some of the flooring.

On the basis of my interior studies of the thick adobe walls and partitions within the Palace and related exploratory findings and recommendations, it soon became the consensus and my purpose to preserve in all integrity, in so far as was possible, all surviving archaeological features and traditions that predated the American Military occupation of August 1846, which was progressively responsible for the vast majority of subsequent modifications.

By far the earliest round-beam or viga-supported ceilings, dating back to about 1700-1750, were closely covered crosswise by split and adzed slabs of pine, upon which an excessive load of earth-fill had been progressively laid to insure drainage; these, due to sagging beams, were completely concealed in several rooms, in which on a wall-to-wall framing below the bottom of the vigas, muslin had been tightly stretched to form a base for ceiling papering. The same muslin treatment had been applied to the adobe plastered walls. Further, traditional Mexican and Pueblo type fireplaces had been replaced with commercial, Colonial type cast-iron equipment with projecting mantels above. These I progressively replaced by conforming Mexican and Pueblo type fireplaces.

With the establishment of the American military forces had also come the first sawmill. [Sawmill: Upper Canyon Road. Later became the home and studio of Mr. Randall Davey. —R.N.] Dimension lumber became available, smooth adobe floors had given way to heavy joist-supported floors covered with wide planking and later with matched and grooved pine. Concurrently the military had begun boxing in, all in the then Colonial style, all doorways, and had enlarged window openings. Most of the supplementary boxing-in was removed as restoration continued and replaced by traditional plaster reveals. By this time the problem of the ceiling rot was solved in my thinking and I began new viga installations only in those rooms where the dry rot and other deterioration forced replacement.

Any building that old and with numerous people going through must have a durable hard-plaster, so we eventually covered all old interior walls with a white hard-finish "yesso" as we progressed with the work of restoration.

While repairing plaster we found other openings, indicating that walls had been disturbed in previous times and obviously some little extension, although how much we could not tell in the plastering, but I knew that in 1866 the west third of this building and the old out-buildings in the rear had to a great extent been demolished and that then extensive remodeling had taken place.

One of the first things Hewett wanted done after we got started was to make plans for descriptive murals. He had been in Denver, and had come away much impressed with murals that artist Carl Lotave had put up in the Indian Room of the New Shirley Savoy Hotel up there. He talked Mr. Frank Springer [Frank Springer, lawyer, palaeontologist and great benefactor of the Museum of New Mexico. —R.N.] into consent to having the Puye and Rito de Los Frijoles rooms and the entrance hall of the old Palace decorated with murals, to show stages or epochs of occupation of the earliest Pueblo Indians, as they had historical relation here. So I kept this in mind.

Arrangements for Lotave to come to Santa Fe were made but he was celebrating too much up there, with the formal opening of the Hotel cafe, bar, and Indian Room, and he did not appear. In frustration Hewett called me early in August 1909 saying: "Bring him down here if you have to rope and tie him and then do everything to get him started and work out spacing of murals, as we have it planned."

My start with Lotave was the Puye room. It already had a level ceiling with good round beams, which I cleaned. In carrying out Hewett's and Lotave's concept of this room, Hewett ordered me to create a false ceiling of dimension-lumber beams, which I lightly blow-torched and suspended below the original. I already had a level ceiling with good beams and I was to work out invisible lights to shine behind Lotave's murals. The old chopping bowls, inverted and inserted in the four corners of this room, he painted to represent Indian pottery. He wanted this design and I finally located these wooden "chopping bowls" at a hardware store, but what a magnificent job he did when he completed the pottery design! When the room was finished it was so oriented that standing in the center you were looking in the four directions, at what you would see. This Puye room was the first one Lotave worked on and in addition I had to look after Lotave himself, the whole time, take him to where he had to make his color sketches; all the while Hewett was urging me to push Lotave.

The last thing Lotave had a habit of religiously doing every night, was get up on a stepladder in the room he was working on. He was still drinking a good deal, so he was pretty shaky and I had to spend time steadying him. About nine p.m. this would commence. It was quite a chore. He made his sketches during the day and I photographed these areas for him so he would get them pictorially correct, in their cardinal directions to the east, west, south and north and properly oriented.

Across the hall and to the west was the room that Governor Curry had used for a while as his bedroom and the little one I used for an office. We had to take out one wall to make a room big enough, for the decision had been made to make it the Rito de Los Frijoles room. Again in this room it was worked out that if you stood out in the very center the cardinal directions would be just as you would see them at the Rito de Los Frijoles, and the important features just as they existed in the four directions. In other words, what was important.

At one place in the center of the room the beams had rotted off so much that not enough support remained, so we had to span one gap to bring it in about four inches, to get new bearings to stabilize those vigas where dry-rot was taking them out. Eventually, it worked out very nicely except in one place where there was a gap, and we had beamed ceilings all the way through the room. I replaced a large section of the north wall in this Ben Hur Room, due to grave deterioration of the wall which had taken place, as a result of settlement and cracks. It was here on September in 1910, that I found buried "en situ" in a thick wall the only very early type corbel, probably previous to 1768, in all my work here. It was atop its post support at one side of an early through entrance from the front of the Palace to its patio. It was doubtless very old. The Urrutia Map, of the "Villa de Santa Fe" was found in the British Museum and sent to me by Miss Barbara Freire-Marreco, of Oxford, England, who had been a student of the School of American Archaeology for several years. The map, although carrying no date, was probably completed before 1768, and shows an inset in the north wall of the Palace of the Governors, the western end of which corresponds almost exactly with the spot where the capital (corbel) were found.

The Ben Hur or Rito de Los Frijoles room at one time in its checkered career was a portal facing on the placita, and the capital (corbel) and column found were part of this. Later, this portal was made over into a room by the simple expedient of building a wall across its front; and incidental to these changes, the capital (corbel) was embedded in this wall and its existence forgotten.

Again I had to take Lotave out to Frijoles and photograph in detail what he was to paint, so he would have these as his guide. At this period he was making his colored sketches here and his shaky mannerisms were growing worse. Whenever he got onto a high point anyplace and have to look down, it was very bad. I ended up roping him. I'd put a secure belt around his waist, then using two ropes, tied one to a tree or good stump and I remained holding the other to quiet his well-founded fear of falling off into the canyon. I'd also had to do this at Puye.

Lotave was about forty years old when here, and an excellent muralist. Mr. Springer became the benefactor of his work. Hewett had become very strong for the artists and also got Springer to put up funds for paintings by Lotave, to represent the historical periods. The first one of these was placed above the main entrance of Palace Avenue, leading into the rear rooms and portraying "The Taking Over at the Time of the American Occupation in Front of the Palace." It showed the Palace as it looked at that time. The other two were hung to its right and left, picturing "The Santa Fe Trail Coming In" and "Indians Before the Coming of the Spanish."

By the end of 1910 the entire frieze for the Puye room, a number of studies related to the environment, and archaeological remains and life-history of the Pajaritan culture were complete. The last three descriptive murals for the entrance of the historical periods ended Lotave's work with the Museum. In all he had been in Santa Fe about one year.

In a front-page article on August 20, 1910, the Santa Fe New Mexican recognized the completion of the Rito de Los Frijoles Room and a reception given its formal opening: "This reception is given under the auspices of the New Mexico Museum's Woman's Auxiliary; the Woman's board of trade form a general reception committee. The Board having given $500 toward the completion of the Rito de Los Frijoles Room, a special committee for that room was elected."

In June 1911, I returned from the second Quirigua expedition and began at once on restoration and repair at the Palace of the Governors, through the generous sum of $2,000 of a number of New Mexico citizens and began the removal of from 1 to 2 feet in depth, the adobe soil from the slabs over the oldest and largest vigas in the front tier of five rooms, replastering and reflooring.

The woefully deteriorated westernmost portion housing the U.S. Post Office had vacated this largest 40' x 34' room and two connecting rooms. I began in this area July 1, 1911 and completed same for use in early September. It had a large thick masonry vault made of limestone that had seen use in early Army days. I promptly got the Penitentiary to remove this. The two small rooms had been used by the Chamber of Commerce. The New Mexico Historical Society's exhibits were in the easternmost-end thereof and in an annoying shambles of disarray.

With 7 to 10 laborers, plasterers and carpenters, plus a few teams at work every day, we stabilized the walls that were ready to fall in and removed from ceilings the usual excessive load of soil cover. At Dr. Hewett's and Mr. Springer's suggestion, of which I approved, I removed the Territorial type doorway and window casings dating after the American occupation.

The old Post Office now becomes our new library, which will house the valuable linguistic library of the late Dr. Franz Nickalaus Finck, of the University of Berlin, which Mr. Springer has recently purchased for the use of the School and will soon be installed. It includes books in some fifty different languages and will afford exceptional facilities for students of language and science. We already have editions of standard works, reports and periodicals on archaeology, ethnology, history and physiography of the Southwest. The school has just gotten out its new bulletin which reads: A registration fee of five dollars is charged. This admits students to all the courses offered, except sketching classes, and entitles one to receive the publications of the School. The cost of board at Santa Fe headquarters (the Palace Hotel), is $12.50 per week, board and room, or one dollar per day for meals; at the Rito de Los Frijoles headquarters (the Elder's Ranch), one dollar per day for meals. The above rates are strictly for those registered with the School of Archaeology. On camping excursions all share the expenses proportionately.

I had been in Washington, D.C. from September 1911 through June 1912, working daytime at the U.S. National Museum, making piece molds and casts of archaeological materials, assisting an Italian expert with casts needed in the upcoming Panama Pacific Exposition at San Diego, California, and attending night classes at George Washington University, pursuant to summer school classes at the University of Colorado at Boulder.

In late August 1912, funds became available, and on return to Santa Fe I began the rehabilitation of the State Historical Society's quarters of five rooms, in the east end of the Palace, where exhibits were housed extending into the entrance hall. By pre-arrangement I added one door at time of restoration. My crew cut an entryway thru the adobe wall that separated the Historical Society's quarters from the Museum and School quarters. Adding this door for purposes of proper exhibit and access purposes made it necessary to carry thru a direct passage from the north tier of rooms, making available access from east to west possible.

Here my initial concern and planning for exhibition rooms was proceeding to my satisfaction. Hewett wanted the cases recessed. Because of great thickness of walls I did not like what he insisted be done and we had to chop into some of these three- and four-foot thick walls. He fretted about not having enough display cases, having seen this done at the Southwest Museum, but we ran into a problem of dust and had a bad time keeping dust out of the cases. We ended up enclosing them in glass and hinged them.

All material meriting reinstalling in the new cases was done. In the early 1900's Governor L. Bradford Prince had promoted a Terita Centennial Celebration [Tertia Centennial: 300 years since the Spanish invasion. —R.N.] and Prince had a canvas stretched over the not yet completed second story of the Federal Building north of town, and there he housed his collection of minerals, largely collected from mining companies, under the canvas tenting.

One of the results of this Tertia Centennial was the formation of the New Mexico Historical Society. After termination of the Centennial the exhibits were taken to the Palace of the Governors and housed in the Historical Society's rooms.

When I was in the process of restoration I removed to the patio the white painted mineral stands and the collections, as I did an exhibit of fraudulent statues, several hundred all told, that the Indians of Cochiti Pueblo had sold to the Governor Prince as authentic Indian gods and relics. Carefully antiqued a bit by burying them in coralles at the pueblo first; then these roughly hewn idols of tufa had found their way to Santa Fe. Later some of them turned up at the Smithsonian Institution for sale. Dr. Neil Judd verified their fraudulence and we decided to dump them. [Dr. Neil Judd: archaeologist and employee of the Smithsonian. —R.N.]

When Governor Prince heard that I had removed the mineral and idol collections, he promptly brought out an injunction against my doing this, but Dr. Hewett and Mr. Springer backed me up, and the collections at my order were moved across the street to the then existing and only partially occupied old Army Officers' barracks.

In 1909, Santa Fe had a population of just under 5,000 persons, of which the majority were Spanish and Mexican Americans, who followed the traditional ways of life and their habits of adobe construction. The threat to the future preservation of the traditional Spanish-Colonial atmosphere of Santa Fe became a matter of increasing concern to a limited and far-seeing segment of Santa Fe's residents, and of vigorous public protest.

As a result the consensus was to hold an "Old-New Santa Fe" exhibit at the Palace, in the big westernmost room. The sum of $1,300 had been raised for this purpose with the city adding $275 more. My part of the effort was to make a ten-foot scaled miniature of the Palace, with the help of Jack Adams, who had so ably assisted me in my restoration of "Balcony House" at the Mesa Verde in 1910. [Jack Adams: Surveyor with the School of Mines, Golden, Colo. —R.N.] We showed the portal restored as I hoped to complete my restoration work here.

In January of 1913, Morley and I left for Yucatan and the Fourth Tropical expedition, this time to make a comprehensive study and photographic record of the ruins of Chichen Itza, Uxmal, plus the city of Merida and movies of native life and scenes of the Henniquin Industry. Morley was working on his report to the Carnegie Institution, from whence sprung their later work in Chichen Itza and I was doing all photography. We ended with an expedition to Cozumel via Mexican gunboat and thence, by renting a small boat, to Tuloom.

I returned, determined to try to restore the last and final phase of the restoration, to which I have devoted so much time and research, which was the restoration of the front portal of the Palace, a non-conforming "gingerbread" piazza type of the 1875 period, consisting of squared-faced posts, to which a varity of moldings were nailed at top and bottom; with the traditional classical portal, prevalent prior to the 1800's.

Hewett said: "No, you have to give that up." I decided to pull a fast one on him and I made the ten-foot scaled model with Jack Adams' help. I had the Urrutia map which gave me authority for the two adobe wings at either end of the portal proper, which shows that the portal at the Palace had two such terminal projections. In smaller buildings, residences and the like, such projections of the house enclosing the ends are frequently present. But such a long portal at one period, as the one at the Palace, which covered the sidewalk of one of the main streets of the city, did not present the feature. The discovery of the Urrutia map, however, effectively settled this point, and indicated that the Palace was no exception to this general type.

I had the corbel I'd found embedded in the front of a north wall of the Palace in 1910, when it was necessary to rebuild the north wall of the former Ben Hur room, which was to become the Rito de Los Frijoles room. To this splendid find of an earlier period I worked it out to conform with more steps to pull it up in size and it worked out well.

When the model was put up, N.B. Laughlin, Judge J.R. McFie, and others of the Board all turned me down, but they reckoned without the public, who saw it and were strong for it and, by gosh, pressure was so great that money was allocated for me to go ahead and build it. The model had achieved its purpose and $3,500 was appropriated by the Board of Regents from current revenues.

I got the large vigas and posts from old Mr. Harrison of Pecos store and lumbering company. They were the fir beams that the Santa Fe Railroad engineers would not accept for the re-timbering of their Raton-Trinidad tunnel. Harrison let me have them at the rail switch just west and south of Pecos Mission. They had the fine character I wanted, and they still stand, firm and strong to the present time. Automobiles have only knocked the bottoms off in places but the two-inch galvanized pipe inserts hold them to their concrete bases. The model had achieved its purpose and in the autumn of 1913 the Palace was restored, as photographically depicted on the cover of the U.S. Postal commemorative stamp of 1960.

The Palace of the Governors, so wonderful in its cyclopean unity of architecture, stands as a tribute to those who long ago planted the standards of Christian culture, beyond the then furthest bounds of civilization. It is in all honesty a Royal House.

EPILOGUE

By 1974, we find history distorted in writings of the Old Palace. The *zaguan* used for storage, which exhibited what existed of historical material in 1882, had been erased in an earlier change, and only crumbling and disarranged rooms were in evidence in 1909. The "puddled walls" so carefully glassed-in to be dust-free to the rooms but left visible to visitors and school-children, so that they could, as Nusbaum thought, view the earliest beginning of this site, are thoughtlessly phased out. The Puye and Rito de Los Frijoles rooms no longer picture the Pajaritan Plateau. The introduction to the "Museum of the Pajaritan Plateau" depicted the "Three Cultures" murals at the entrance, so carefully executed by the genius of artist Carl Lotave, are gone. The desire of the Legislature of 1909 had been to promote understanding of the cultures of the Pajarito.

In 1974 I walked into the Palace to view once again the three-culture murals by Lotave at the entrance and seeing only bare walls, I walked to the desk to ask the attending lady where I might view again the Lotave murals of the Three-Cultures that once hung here. She looked at me blankly and asked: "Who was Carl Lotave?" Ah, history!

92

BRIEF CHRONOLOGY OF THE PALACE OF THE GOVERNORS

1610   Built (probably) as the main structure of the "Casas Reales" in New Mexico's new capital.

1680   Occupied by the Pueblo Indians after they had driven the Spaniards from Santa Fe.

1693   Reoccupied by the Spaniards.

1807   Lt. Zebulon Pike, U.S. Army, imprisoned in the Palace jail.

1822   Mexican Independence. No longer the "Royal Palace."

1837   Jose Gonzales, a Taos Indian, installed as Governor, during the short-lived insurrection; soon after he was executed.

1846   Occupied by Stephen Watts Kearney, U.S. Army, Aug. 18th.

1862   Occupied for two months by invading Confederate Army from Texas.

1866   West third of the building and old out-buildings in the rear demolished. Next two years saw them extensively remodeled.

1869   James L. Collins, U.S. Depository, found dead in office in west end of the Palace, and safe robbed.

1870   Mexican and Spanish archives, in Palace since 1693, were sold by Governor Pile as scrap paper.

1878-   General Lew Wallace wrote part of Ben Hur story in the Palace. Room
1881   then called Ben Hur Room.

1900   Palace given up as the Capital, new Capital building completed in Santa Fe. Still used as Post Office for a time and some private offices.

1909   Palace restored, to become first unit of the Museum of New Mexico.

From the Santa Fe *New Mexican*. August 20, 1911.

RECEPTION AT THE PALACE

The reception given last evening under the auspices of the New Mexico Museum, in the Palace of the Governors in honor of archaeologists and other scientists, students of the School of American Archaeology, visitors in the city and staff and faculty was a splendid success. Although announced as informal it had all the brilliance of the reception of last year and the attendance was even greater.

The setting could not have been more appropriate for such an occasion, for the Old Palace rooms seemed mellow with the romance of past ages. The pictures of the ancient cliffs of the Puye and in the delightful Rito were lit up by shaded electric bulbs, and visitors were transported in fancy, back to the days of the ancient civilization.

It was a study of this civilization which was the motif back of the efforts of so many distinguished men and women who attended the reception and whose presence attested the important role Old Santa Fe is playing in the scientific world.

The reception began at 8:30 P.M. when automobiles and hacks hurried up to the Old Palace which was ablaze with many lights. The various rooms and the hall were decorated in a most charming manner. In the assembly room were cut flowers and golden rod, and in the Puye room in which the refreshments were served were masses of dahlias and nasturtia. The table was decorated with golden rod. In the hall leading to this room stood the tall, stately hollyhock which seemed singularly appropriate.

The receiving line stood in the assembly room. In it were Dr. Edgar L. Hewett, director of the School of American Archaeology, Governor and Mrs. William J. Mills, Miss Alice Cunningham Fletcher, and Hon. John R. McFie, Associate Justice of the Supreme Court of New Mexico.

This was the first social affair held in the restored East Room of the Old Palace, formerly the post office of Santa Fe, and before that the office of the disbursing agent of the military post. The work of restoration has been beautifully done by the staff of the museum which adhered rigidly to the old architecture of two or three centuries ago. Special admiration was given to the immense viga which supports the ceiling and which was carved after the model found imbedded in the walls of the Palace. The supporting pillars are immense tree trunks taken from the nearby forests and in whose limbs but two months ago the birds were singing.

Among those seen at this function were Miss Alice Fletcher probably the greatest woman ethnologist in the world and who is the guest of Miss Conrad and Miss Olsen, while she is in the city; F.W. Hodge, Chief of the Bureau of Ethnology of Washington and well known through the land; Dr. L.B. Paton of the Hartford Theological Seminary and a noted authority on Semitic history and literature; former Congressman John F. Lacey of Iowa, who has done more than any living legislator for archaeology; R.W. Corwin, the distinguished physician and surgeon and scientist from Pueblo; Dr. Mitchell Carroll, of Washington, a noted lecturer and secretary of the American Institute of Archaeology; T. La Flesche, the greatest of living Indian ethnologists, from Oklahoma; Edgar Wells, administrator and former acting dean of Harvard University, and many others.

From Santa Fe were many men and women prominent in the political and social world. In fact, there were enough "lions" in the assembly to have made notable half a dozen salons in Paris.

After refreshments were served in the Puye room, the first Regiment band, which had discoursed music in the Rito room to the great delight of everyone present, proceeded to the assembly room and began a dreamy waltz. That marked the end of the reception and the beginning of the dance which swept over the new, polished floor in a room which probably was witnessing its first dance in all its three hundred years of existence.

REFERENCES

BOOKS

Burns, Walter Noble. *The Saga of Billy the Kid.* Doubleday and Co., 1926.

Davis. W.W.H. *El Gringo, or New Mexico and Her People.* Rydal Press, 1938.

Driggs, Howard R. *Westward America.* Trails Edition, 1942.

Gibson, George Rutledge. *Journal of a Soldier under Kearney and Doniphan, 1846-1847.* Ed. by Ralph P. Bieber. The Arthur H. Clark Co., 1935.

Gregg, Josiah. *Commerce of the Prairies.* University of Oklahoma Press, 1954.

Hayden, F.V. *U.S. Geological and Geographical Survey of the Territories.* Washington, Government Printing Office, 1870.

Narrative of a Journey in the Prairie, 1831. Vol. 4. Arkansas Historical Society.

New Mexico. American Guide Series, 1940.

Southwest on the Turquoise Trail. Ed. by Archer Butler Hulbert. The Stewart Commission of Colorado College and the Denver Public Library, 1933.

Villagra, Gaspar Perez de. *Historia del Nuevo Mejico.* Trans. by Gilberto Espinosa. Quivira Society, 1933.

ARTICLES, PAPERS, BULLETINS, LEGISLATION

Anderson, Clinton P. "The Adobe Palace." *New Mexico Historical Review,* April 1944.

Bulletin of the Archaeological Institute of American; Second Annual Report, 1908-1909. School of American Research.

Bulletin of New Mexico Normal University, No. 11, January 1908.

Institute of American Archaeology, Papers of. Dec. 31, 1908, Toronto.

Hewett, Edgar L. *Papers of the School of American Research,* 1938.

"An Act for the Preservation of American Antiquities" (Lacey Bill). *Journal of American Archaeology,* Vol. XI (1907); Vol. XII (1908).

"An' Act to establish a museum for the Territory of New Mexico," Amended House Bill No. 100. Territorial Legislature of New Mexico.

Kiva, The. Journal of the Arizona Archaeological and Historical Society, Vol. 25, No. 4, April 1960.

Mogollon, Gen. Juan Ignacio Flores. "Report to Gov. Felix Martinez on the condition of the Palace of the Governors at Santa Fe." Trans. Ralph E. Twitchell. New Mexico Archive No. 253.

New Mexican, The Santa Fe. Dec. 2, 1873; Dec. 9, 1873; and Aug. 20, 1911.

Nusbaum, Jesse L. Notes, 1907-1975 (unpublished).

School of American Research, Papers of, 1925. ("The Fiesta Book.")

www.ingramcontent.com/pod-product-compliance
Lightning Source LLC
LaVergne TN
LVHW091204080426
835509LV00006B/824